Building Electronic Library Collections

The Essential Guide to Selection Criteria and Core Subject Collections

Diane Kovacs

Neal-Schuman Publishers, Inc.

New York   London

Published by Neal-Schuman Publishers, Inc.
100 Varick Street
New York, NY 10013

The paper used in this publication meets minimum requirements of American National Standard for Information Sciences—Permanence of Paper for Printed Library Materials, ANSI Z39, 48–1992.

Printed and bound in the United States of America.

ISBN: 1–55570–362–3

Library of Congress Cataloging-in-Publication Data

Kovacs, Diane.
    Building electronic library collections : the essential guide to selection
criteria and core subject collections / Diane Kovacs.
        p.   cm.
    Includes bibliographical references and index.
    ISBN 1–55570–362–3
    1. Libraries—United States—Special collections—Electronic information
resources. I. Title.

Z692.C65 K68 2000
025.2'84—dc21   99–048575

Contents

Contents

List of Tables and Figures

Tables

Figures

Table of E-library Builder Stories

Foreword

Just three short years ago, I began the work of editing a collection of works on Internet sources for reference work. Some of the sites referenced were actually telnet or Gopher sites that could be accessed via the Web. Since then a myriad of government, commercial, and educational sites have been added to the Web making some of those original sites diminish in centrality to reference. Additionally, some of those sites have moved or disappeared—which everyone predicted would happen when trying to pin down the Web in a print publication. Many of those original sites remain valid and will still be referenced in a publication such as this. I don't believe any Gopher or telnet sites remain as core resources.

It is expected in this furious time of online publication and transitioning from legacy technologies to Web technologies that any work which aims to assist professionals with electronic literature will need to be revised, expanded, and refined . . . all at the same time.

Building Electronic Library Collections is an important step forward for library professionals. This publication not only identifies sites for library reference collections, it winnows out those that are less central and, more importantly, provides a taxonomic structure familiar to our print collections and our traditions in organizing reference material.

In 1997 it was enough to eliminate sites that were unreliable in availability, suspect in content and origination, or simply not appropriate in a reference environment (just as most books do not belong in a reference collection). Now librarians are in the enviable position of choosing not to add items to a collection purely because they do not fit the scope of interest of users . . . not because there is anything inherently wrong with the sites. It is no longer enough for reference folk to bookmark or add links to their pages for every site that has helped them answer a reference question. Increasingly, a more deliberate and scientific approach to collecting electronic sites is required. Budgets and shelf space are usually the driving forces for libraries to keep selection of books and print journals a deliberate process. Relevancy, time, clutter, and unnecessary duplication of effort are increasingly becoming the driving forces in making electronic collection development a deliberate process.

Building Electronic Library Collections' approach of combining core sites with important metasites to assist librarians in the selection process is a sound one. Librarians love to quote Samuel Johnson's "Knowledge is of two kinds: we know a subject ourselves, or we know where we can find information upon it." Metasites lead us to all those great places that are simply too vast to bookmark. Reference with a print collection is done by understanding a classification system, understanding the various publication types, and knowing when to turn to other collections or references for questions so specific they are not housed in general sources. Kovacs has moved those principals to the digital environment and provides a map for collecting and storing electronic information so that information professionals and users can easily retrieve those sites. Additionally, the case studies interspersed throughout the book illuminate real life ways of collecting and organizing sites, as well as illustrate that we have much to learn from each other about how to approach this task.

This publication focuses on the process of preparing the reference environment, by preparing one's electronic shelves for easy and ready access. It is a different approach than I took two years ago in the midst of a more hectic and fragmented reality. Then it was hard to know at first glance if the Web was even a worthwhile tool to pursue for certain questions, thus causing me to fashion a book that would help "on the spot". While some will still criticize a print attempt at taming the Web for the library environment, it is necessary that we do so to allow a variety of approaches to reach our minds and shape our visioning, planning, and thinking skills. *Building Electronic Library Collections* is an indispensable tool for planning and refining our digital reference environments.

Karen R. Diaz
Web Librarian, Ohio State University Libraries and Editor, *Reference Sources on the Internet: Off the Shelf and Onto the Web*

Preface

An electronic library is a collection of information resources electronically formatted from a variety of resources including the Internet and the Web. *Building Electronic Library Collections: The Essential Guide to Selection Criteria and Core Subject Collections* is specifically concerned with those Web-based resources that librarians "collect" with a particular user group in mind. Physically, electronic libraries (or *e-libraries* for short) usually appear as a compilation of links on a Web page or site maintained by a library. As such, the simplest definition of an e-library is "a Web-published collection of Web-based resources." The e-library is distinct from the digitial library (commonly defined as a collection of full-text materials created from print or holographic primary documents or artifacts) and the virtual library (a term generally perceived as offering services as well as resources).

Developing an e-library is an ambitious project for any library because the building process attempts to recreate an essential of what most users conceive of as "the" library—its collection—in virtual space. Librarians undertake these projects for many reasons. Sowards' (1998) description of why we do this is the most precise and concise I have yet encountered. Although his specific point-of-reference is reference sites on the Web, his points are equally applicable to any e-library project. He says that:

> Librarians invest time and resources in creating reference Websites because doing so extends four familiar library service functions into cyberspace:
> - *Selection:* Users who can rely on reference Websites save significant time by avoiding inefficient, inconclusive Web surfing.
> - *Endorsement:* Librarians implicitly vouch for the quality of the linked sources: their relevance for solving a given problem, their consistent availability, and the accuracy and currency of their content.
> - *Organization:* A well-designed site allows users to move rapidly and accurately among a large number of Websites, finding a high proportion of relevant resources.
> - *Cooperation:* These sites allow experienced librarians to share their knowledge of the Web with each other and with users, at all times of the day and irrespective of distance. (p. 3)

Other benefits of building an e-library include: enhancing existing services to core user groups; providing new services to core user groups; attracting new library users; and providing new (or better) services to users who are reluctant (or find it difficult) to come into the physical library.

Building Electronic Library Collections is intended for any librarian who wants to begin developing or expanding an e-library. It is intended to serve two distinct purposes. First of all, it is a collection planning guide specifically written for collecting, evaluating, and selecting Web-based information resources. A collection development plan is just as essential for creating a good e-library as it is for building a collection of print resources. As it would for physical collections, such a plan for e-library collections must consider users' needs and establish selection criteria. Second, the book identifies core collections within major subject areas collected by most libraries.

Chapter One, "Developing an Electronic Library Collection on the Web" begins with a brief review of the e-library collection development literature and then presents a framework within which librarians can plan and develop e-libraries. Specific strategies are recommended for collecting, evaluating, and selecting Web-based information resources.

Chapters Two through Seven are each devoted to a specific subject or type of information resource. Each chapter identifies specific evaluation criteria and recommends a core collection within the subject area of focus. Chapter Two covers ready-reference materials. Chapter Three covers business, jobs, and employment information. Chapter Four contains information on health and medicine resources. Chapter Five examines legal information resources. Chapter Six covers biological sciences, social sciences, and technology. Chapter Seven covers education, current awareness, and readers advisory as well as resources for print and other collection activities.

Because building e-libraries requires good Web searching skills and the ability to create basic Web pages (or at least to understand the basic concepts underlying Web page construction). The first covers basic and advanced Web searching; the second covers basic Web page construction using a simple HTML editor. Both of these are also accessible on the companion Web page as Web-based tutorials. The Webliographies, bibliographies, and the core ready-reference e-libraries from each chapter are available as continuously updated and revised Web pages on the companion Website at www.neal-schuman.com/elibrary.html. This site is password protected. The login name and password are: *egreader*; *neal2schuman*.

In many ways, those who build e-library builders today are taking the best principles of traditional library collection development and applying them to virtual resources. *Building Electronic Library Collections* can serve as a resource for clarifying how the collection development process translates to the Web environment, as a guide for developing selection criteria for specific subject areas, and as collection of carefully selected resources for starting or expanding an e-library collection.

Readers are encouraged to bookmark the companion Website mentioned earlier in this preface. The Website will be continually updated as the sites identified in these print pages move or expire and new, even better sites are developed. Readers are also encouraged to send feedback on the sites chosen for inclusion in the core collection—and suggestions for expanding it—to diane@kovacs.com.

Print or Electronic Works Cited in This Preface

Sowards, S.W. 1998. "A Typology for Ready Reference Web Sites in Libraries." *First Monday* 1, no. 14: (www.firstmonday.dK/).

Acknowledgments

Thank you very very much to Charles Harmon. This project would have been impossible without his wise support and patience. Thank you to my husband Michael J. Kovacs who tried to make sure I had some time off. My assistant, Molly Parsson, was essential in getting the Webliographies and bibliographies organized, HTMLed, and online. Angela Elkordy provided continuous professional feedback and supplied me with copies of many of the articles and book chapters I've cited. Karen Diaz re-designed the Webliography and Core Library Web pages within a tight deadline as well as writing the foreword. Kara Robinson supplied sympathy and emergency copies of articles I needed. Also thank you as always to all the wonderful production and client service folks at Neal-Schuman, especially Jose Aboy. A special thank you goes to the anonymous reviewer who reviewed the draft manuscript for Neal-Schuman during the summer of 1999. This individual brought many excellent resources to my attention and the critique they provided improved the book immeasurably.

Introduction

> "While the principles of collection development, which were developed in the world of print publications, do not change radically with new publishing technologies, methods of decision making and specific selection guidelines must be adjusted significantly to incorporate new publishing formats." (p. 71.)
>
> **Demas, S. G. 1994. "Collection Development for the Electronic Library: A Conceptual and Organizational Model."**
> ***Library Hi Tech* 12, no 3:71-80.**

The environment in which libraries operate has changed dramatically in the past decade. The ubiquity of microcomputers and the publication of information on and through the Internet and the World Wide Web (the Web) have resulted in imperatives for libraries to begin Internet information resource collections for their clients. Evidence of professional awareness of this imperative can be found in the Special Libraries Association document "Competencies for Special Librarians of the 21st Century" (www.sla.org/conf/final/competent.html):

> The Special Librarian . . .
> 1.6 uses appropriate information technology to acquire, organize, and disseminate information. . . . Provides a support service for electronic information service users. Keeps up-to-date with new electronic information products and modes of information delivery.

The Web provides one of the best solutions for a user interface through which to develop electronic libraries (e-libraries) and a platform to make them available.

Learning from past experiences of other libraries who have developed strategies for collecting Internet resources and constructing e-libraries is a recurring theme throughout this book. The specific resources that are selected and how they are organized will be unique for each library.

In 1993, I began construction of an e-library of Internet resources for the Reference Department of the Kent State University Libraries. The e-library was made available via a Gopher server running on an Apple Macintosh with a network connection to the Kent State University campus Internet backbone (Gopher being the more used technology in those early days of the Web). Everything about the Internet was new to the library staff. We began, logically enough, by developing a collection plan and providing Internet training for every subject specialist in the library. Our intention was that each subject specialist, as part of their regular collection activities, would also collect Internet resources for our Gopher e-library. The subject organization of our e-library was based upon the core subject areas taught at the University. The resources we included were representative of everything from architecture to nursing, fresh water/Great Lakes biology to English, foreign language to literature, and computer science to liquid crystal engineering. We also included local files with information about library hours and services. At the same time the library began making inter-library loan request forms available through the campus mainframe. Eventually, I received grant funding from the university to hire a graduate student to do the actual inputting of resource links into the Gopher server. The topic of collecting and evaluating Internet resources began to be very interesting to librarians at about that time. Members of our team were invited to speak and write articles (see historical materials at www.kovacs.com/dianevita.html#pubs and www.kovacs.comdianevita.html# conf) about our strategies for collection and evaluation of Internet. The Gopher e-library that we built has been extinct since 1997, replaced by a state-wide Web-based union catalog and e-library system (OHIOLINK— www.ohiolink.edu or see also Dannelly [1997]). A copy of our first Internet resource collection-planning document is reproduced in this introduction. This historic e-library example is the first E-Library Builder Story of several that are included in this book. E-Library Builder Stories of actual e-library collection development projects are used in each chapter to illustrate different phases of e-library creation and subject area collection development. Stories were chosen to represent different types of libraries including school, public, academic and special libraries, and regional library organization. The coverage of the stories is international, but limited to English language sites. There are literally hundreds of stories that could have been included. See The WWW Library Directory (www.webpan.com/msauers/libdir/) or Libweb (http:// sunsite.berkeley.edu/Libweb/) for a list of 3,000 libraries worldwide with a Web presence of some kind.

● ●

E-library Builder Story

Library and Information Sciences Gopher Server Resource Collection Development Policies and Strategies

I. History

In the past, selections have been made by the Library and Information Sciences Gopher Server administrators. Input was requested from reference librarians on the structure and naming of the menus. Reference librarians were asked to recommend resources and to verify the value of resources selected by the Library and Information Sciences Gopher Server administrators.

The Library and Information Sciences Gopher Server administrators used e-conferences such as Library and Information Sciences Gopher Server Jewels, NEWNIR-L (new network resources announcement), and Net-Happenings to gather all the newly announced Gopher accessible (mainly telnet, wais, and Gopher sites) resources. In addition, both Library and Information Sciences Gopher Server administrators monitored subject specific discussions for resources in the humanities and social sciences.

Resources were evaluated by the Library and Information Sciences Gopher Server administrators on the main criteria of: Is the resource of interest to students, faculty, and staff at Kent State University given our curriculum and research interests of the faculty? This evaluation was usually based on the name or title of the resource and occasionally through actual connection to the resource for review.

From the beginning any librarian could make a recommendation and the resources recommended were added to the Library and Information Sciences Gopher Server as quickly as possible by the Library and Information Sciences Gopher Server administrators.

II. Plans for the Future

As a result of the significant growth of resources on the Internet, issues have been raised concerning quality and usefulness of Internet resources. As a strategy for responding to such issues, it would serve our clients well if we could formally introduce Internet resources into the collection development activities of each subject liaison in the library.

Subject liaisons would be asked to monitor for and forward to the Library and Information Sciences Gopher Server administrators the information for any resources that would be useful in their subject area. The Library and Information Sciences Gopher Server admininstrators could offer training on Internet resource identification strategies.

Ideally, staff or student staff could be assigned the task of monitoring NEWNIR-L and Library and Information Sciences Gopher Server Jewels and forwarding announcements for new resources to subject liaisons for their evaluation much in the same way as we do now with Choice cards. The Library and Information Sciences Gopher Server administrators would keep the responsibility of physically adding the resources to the Library and Information Sciences Gopher Server. Resources requiring subscription or licensing fees would be referred to the Acquisitions Department and appropriate Liaisons for review.

Eventually it might be possible to include the departmental representatives in the Internet resource evaluation and recommendation process.

Print or Electronic Works Cited in the Introduction

Author

Dannelly, G. N. 1997. "Cooperation is the Future of Collection Management and Development: OhioLINK and CIC." In *Collection Management for the 21st Century*. Westport, Conn.: Greenwood Press.

Demas, S. G. 1994. "Collection Development for the Electronic Library: A Conceptual and Organizational Model." *Library Hi Tech* 12, no 3:71–80.

Websites Cited in the Introduction

The WWW Library Directory (www.webpan.com/msauers/libdir/)
Libweb (http://sunsite.berkeley.edu/Libweb/)

1
Developing an Electronic Library Collection on the Web

"Collection development (also known as collection or materials management) involves the identification, selection, acquisition, and evaluation of a collection of library resources (e.g. print materials, audiovisual materials, electronic resources) for a community of users. While it is the goal of collection development to meet the information needs of everyone in a user community, this is not usually realized due to financial constraints, the diversity of user information needs, and the vast amount of information. Nonetheless, public libraries strive to provide the greatest number of library resources to meet the information and recreational needs of the majority of their user community within the confines of fiscal realities."

From Collection Development Training for Arizona Public Libraries.
www.dlapr.lib.az.us/cdt/index.htm

Introduction

Today, being an effective librarian in any type of library—public, academic, or special—means expanding the range of resources that you provide for library clients to include those available in electronic format. Librarians must have one foot in the nineteenth century—books, manuscripts, print journals, and archives—and one foot in the twenty-first century—databases, electronic journals, electronic texts, electronic correspondences, and electronically stored archives of all types. The pattern of our professional activities is still recognizably similar to what it has been for the last half century. We still collect, evaluate, and organize information resources. Our roles as librarians are becoming focused on providing clients with the information they need, when they need it, where they need it, and organizing that information for logical access by our clients. Whether we are reference librarians, collection development librarians, bibliographers, or catalogers, our jobs are much more proactive with clients than they have ever been before.

In 1994 Demas predicted the profound effect that electronic publications would have on libraries. His plan to cope was to incorporate the selection and acquisition of electronic resources into the traditional collection development responsibilities of librarians regardless of their technical knowledge. However, he advocates having specialists in the technologies and specific selection criteria required to make the electronic publications accessible.

Collection development of Internet resources for a Web-based e-library can be based on the same basic collection policy as traditional resources. Most libraries have devoted considerable time to developing collections of materials that best serve their communities of clients. There are, of course, some unique criteria related to the Web-based format of the electronic resources. Selection is simply a process of comparing individual resources with criteria of collection development policy, evaluating the quality, then determining the relevancy of the resource to the information needs of your clients.

Demas (1994) stated the need for adjustments to collection development principles in order to integrate electronic formats:

> Electronic publishing has profound implications for collection development, which is defined as the intentional and systematic building of the set of information resources to which the library provides access. While the principles of collection development, which were developed in the world of print publications, do not change radically with new publishing technologies, methods of decision making and specific selection guidelines must be adjusted significantly to incorporate new publishing formats. (p. 71).

The Internet has increased access to many types of information resources that previously were difficult or expensive to obtain. Increasingly, more traditional types of information like newspapers, newsletters, journals, books, dissertations, bibliographic databases, and even television and radio news information are being made accessible on the Internet. Some are even published directly to the Internet instead of, or in advance of, print versions. Resources once only available locally in libraries or agencies are now accessible globally; such as government information, community or campus specific information, or library catalogs. The Internet also makes possible the sharing of resources between libraries so that the expense of database products can be shared as well.

Kuny and Cleveland (1998) point out one of the myths which the general public accepts about the Internet which justifies the intervention of librarians:

> Myth 1. The Internet is the Digital Library . . . In reality the Internet and the World Wide Web are to libraries what a flea market is to the Library of Congress. For many common library requests, locating information on the Internet remains highly inefficient compared to traditional library sources . . . Finding information is difficult, the quality of the information is quite variable, and reliable, professional assistance for the confused and lost is lacking. (p. 107).

Another analogy we might use is that the Internet is like the shelves that we fill with organized books/information products. The Web is an information product supplier. We must select what we want to organize on our own e-library shelves.

Review of Recent Internet Resource Collection Development Literature

In 1995, Demas, McDonald, Lawrence, and Piontek and Garlock, were some of the first librarians to discuss practical guidelines for collection development of Internet resources as opposed to the mainly theoretical discussions of previous publications. Piontek and Garlock's article is primarily a Webliography/Gopherography of collection development tools. Technology and site lists are out-of-date but the evaluation section has some nice points.

A main theme of the Demas et al. (1995) discussion is that collection of Internet resources can and should use the same collection criteria as more traditional resources. The "Taxonomy of Internet Resources" introduced by Demas et al. has been used by subsequent researchers and as a practical guide by many librarians. The taxonomy is adapted later in the "Developing a Collection Plan for the Web-Based E-Library" section of this chapter. Demas et al. also clarify the analogous relationships between Internet resources and other types of resource formats:

> Although electronic retrieval and network delivery of Internet resources changes the way information is stored and manipulated, traditional collection development concepts, principles and practices were found to apply equally to Internet selection. For example, while the text of an electronic book can be downloaded, reprinted, graphically enhanced, keyword searched, or even rewritten for that matter, from a collection manager's perspective, the title is still a monograph, no different than its print counterpart. (p. 281).

Norman (1997), Fedunok (1997), Yochelson, et al. (1997) and Coutts (1998) have all thoroughly reviewed the literature relating collection development of electronic resources in general and Internet resources in particular. Norman's article is the report of a study which surveyed 15 Midwestern academic libraries on their handling of electronic information sources in their collection development policies and practices. It is very useful as it not only surveyed for the handling of commercial electronic resources such as CD-ROM, but also of Internet resources. Another useful aspect of his study is that Norman used the Demas et al. (1995) article to guide his survey. He asked if the libraries had been "mainstreaming" collection development of Internet resources. He found that 73 percent had been "mainstreaming" development of Internet resources and the rest planned to. Demas et al. (1995) discussed their definition of "mainstreaming":

> To achieve the "mainstreaming," or integration of electronic formats, we must develop the staff skills in selecting, cataloging, and providing service with these publications. For example, we must buy the equipment and build the necessary computing and telecommunications infrastructure to handle a variety of electronic publications; and we must learn to educate our patrons in their use. (p. 72).

Norman also asked—based on the Demas et al. article—about whether libraries were training their subject specialists to use the Internet for collection development. Seventy-three percent reported that they were training specialists and the rest either reported that they planned to or did not answer the question. He also found that 93 percent of the libraries surveyed had developed a taxonomy of electronic resources similar to the one described by Demas et al.

In addition to her excellent review of the literature prior to 1997, Fedunok's (1997) article also provides a synthesis of 18 library electronic resource collection policy statements. Yochelson et al. (1997) is a handbook for Library of Congress "Recommending Officers." Yochelson et al. (1997) review the practical literature up to 1997 and also describe the collection tools that were extant for use in collecting Internet resources. Most of those tools still exist but have relocated since publication of the handbook. Coutts (1998) is a kind of "state of the profession" report on collection development and electronic resources for research collections in the United Kingdom.

Rosenfeld, Janes, and Vander Kolk (1995); Morville and Wickhorst (1996); Rioux (1997); and Tennant (1998) all argue well for the development of "subject guides" or "subject bibliographies" as the proper role for librarians in ameliorating access to Internet resources for our clients. Rioux's metaphor of e-library collection development as "hunting and gathering in cyberspace" is an amusing and useful way to think about the process. She says:

> Over the centuries librarians have pretty much gotten a handle on building collections of resources in the physical media like print and film. There are review journals, the publishing industry is well-organized, and subscription agents are always happy to help keep things neat and tidy. It's a little like agriculture, where the farmer/librarian goes into a well-tended field to harvest a crop of known type and quality. Developing a collection of Internet, especially World Wide Web, resources is another situation altogether. It's much more like foraging in the jungle; a trackless, vine-tangled wilderness full of unknown species, some of which look appetizing but may be poi-

sonous and others of which look drab and unappealing but may well be the most nourishing. The librarian collecting electronic resources is not a harvester of cultivated crops but a hunter and gatherer of wild fruits and other treasures. (p. 130).

Finally, Kuny and Cleveland (1998) and Kopp (1997) inject a note of warning. Kuny and Cleveland identify their article as a provocation; then they go on to give the darkest picture possible saying that a "call-to-arms is needed in the library community to meet the challenges of digital libraries—and we must attempt to recognize these challenges clearly. (p. 107). Their discussion of the problems regarding copyright and information access is cogent and one of the most realistic, informed discussions to date. Despite their very real concerns about the difficulties involved with making information available through digital libraries, Kuny and Cleveland have a clearly positive view of the role librarians should be playing:

Technological progress has changed how libraries do their work, not why. But the most profound technological development, a connection of computer to computer in an unbroken chain around the world, may alter the fundamental concept of the library in the twenty-first century. But, we would suggest that technology will not substantially alter the business of librarians—connecting people with information. (p. 107).

Kopp (1997) "The Politics of a Virtual Collection" writes very realistically about the politics within libraries, between libraries, and between libraries and their organizations or governmental environment. He points out that there is more to creating e-libraries cooperatively than just doing the e-library construction. We must also work cooperatively with each other and within our political spheres. He says:

Seeking to understand the politics of the virtual collection and to learn how to work with the political process at all levels will aid considerably in the realization of the virtual collection. Without that effort and accomplishment, the virtual collection is very likely to remain a utopian vision.

Learning from what other e-library builders have already done is the best strategy to follow in planning your own e-library project. At this stage in the development of e-libraries there is no need for anyone to recreate the wheel and try to create their e-library from scratch as it were. As discussed in the Introduction stories of e-library builders are used in each chapter to illustrate different phases of e-library creation and subject area collection development.

The e-library builder stories represent school (Taft Middle School), public (Columbus Metropolitan Libraries, San Bernardino County Public Libraries), academic (Cyberstacks, InfoMine, LII, University of Canterbury), special libraries (Pinakes), and regional library organizations (OPLIN, MEL). Other e-library builder stories will appear periodically on the companion Website at www.neal-schuman.com.

Preliminary Planning for the Web-based E-library

Basically, you must plan how to collect, evaluate, and select all the resources that you want to include in your e-library and organize them on Web pages, or in a database accessible through a Web page, and publish them on a Web server. There are a few preliminary planning questions that will be helpful to address before beginning to collect resources for a Web-based e-library. For the most part the preliminary questions relate to the time and commitment of personnel to the task of e-library construction. Some of these are basic technology questions. Other than general considerations, the technology used for e-libraries is out of the scope for this book. However, several recent publications including Stielow, Frederick, (Ed.) (1999) and Rosenfeld (1998), as well as some of the other publications mentioned in the bibliography cover e-library technical issues in more depth. The discussion list Web4lib@ sunsite.berkeley.edu with archives at http://sunsite.berkeley.edu/Web4Lib/ archive.html serves as the primary in-depth, Web-based e-library technical information source for many librarians. Use the *Directory of Scholarly and Professional Electronic Conferences* (through www.arl.org/scomm/edir/) or the PHOAKS project (www.phoaks.com) to find other technical discussion groups for Web-based e-libraries.

The most important planning questions are:

1. Is an Internet-connected computer running Web server software already available through your organization?
2. What computer hardware and Web server software will need to be purchased or otherwise acquired? What will it cost? How will it be funded?
3. Are personnel available that are knowledgeable enough to produce and maintain an e-library by collecting, evaluating, and selecting resources and incorporating them into a Website?
4. How much time do you estimate that responsible individuals will be able to commit to the planning, collecting, evaluating and selecting Internet resources, construction, and maintenance of the e-library?
5. How many people will be needed to plan, collect, evaluate, and select Internet resources and then to maintain the e-library?

Is an Internet-connected Computer Running Web Server Software Already Available Through Your Organization?

Just ask. If your organization has a systems department, ask them. If your organization is affiliated with a library system, you might ask them about using any Web server that they make available. Most of the libraries in our e-library builder stories had organizational access to an Internet-connected computer running a Web server. Many e-library projects have been developed without the need for additional support or funding because the library already has access to a Web server through the institution that they serve. The San Bernardino County Library's e-library, for example, is run from the San Bernardino County government's Web server. Another example is Cyberstacks, which is provided through the Iowa State University's campus Web server.

What Computer Hardware and Web Server Spotware Will Need to be Purchased or Otherwise Acquired? What Will It Cost? How Will It be Funded?

If you find you'll need to acquire computers, an Internet connection, and server software, you'll need to investigate costs and funding. Many states are providing grant money to schools and public libraries for Internet projects. Some library grant funding agency sites and companies that provide funding to support school and library Internet projects and other projects can be searched for at the Community of Science site at www.cos.com. If you have at least a basic Internet connection you can use Web search tools to search for other sources of grants and funding information on the Internet. For example, the Librarians' Index to the Internet (LII) is hosted by the University of California at Berkeley's SunSITE project which is funded in part by Sun Microsystems (http://sunsite.berkeley.edu/).

Are There Personnel Available Who Have the Knowledge Needed to Produce and Maintain an E-library by Collecting, Evaluating, and Selecting Resources and Incorporating Them Into a Website?

The people who collect, evaluate, select, and organize the links will require basic and advanced Web searching and resource evaluation skills (see the "Information Evaluation Criteria and Their Practical Application to Internet Information" section of this chapter). Knowledge of simple HTML elements and the URL format will be helpful for them as well. Those who create the Web pages will need to know how to author Web pages with HTML or an HTML editor (see Companion Website).

It has been pointed out by several authors previously cited that the collection of Internet resources will be more efficient if the individuals chosen to collect resources in particular subject areas have some background in those subjects. Expertise will be meaningful when the resources are evaluated and selected for inclusion in the e-library. Nearly all of the e-libraries described in the e-library builder stories recruited individuals with subject expertise to select Internet resources in their area.

Depending on your choice or the availability of a computer platform, Web server software and Website design may require computer professionals who are able to administer the computer system and Web server. In some cases you'll want a computer professional or other trained individual who is able to do CGI (Common Gateway Interface), database, or other types of programming in Perl, C, or other programming languages. Programmers will not be needed for simple HTML-based Websites. However, if your e-library will access databases in response to searches, or will offer certain other types of interactivity, a programmer with at least basic programming skills will be needed.

How Much Time do You Estimate that Responsible Individuals Will be Able to Commit to the Planning, Collecting, Evaluating, and Selecting of Internet Resources, Construction, and Maintenance of the E-library?

Constructing e-libraries is very time consuming. Do you have staff who can spend time planning and implementing the e-library? Will you seek volunteers to assist in its construction and maintenance? Will you do all the work yourself? Will individuals be able to use paid "on-the-job" time or will work be done on unpaid personal time? The Taft Middle School e-library was created during unpaid personal time, but maintenance takes place during librarian Deb Logan's working hours. The LII is maintained by volunteers, with the coordinator being paid by an LSTA grant for time spent managing the e-library. The Cyberstacks project was created and maintained under tenure-track conditions, where Gerry McKiernan was using research and personal time to develop and maintain the project.

Obviously, the more comprehensive you intend your e-library collection to be, the more time will be required. A small subject-focused e-library collection might take only a few hours. For example, for a workshop for the Columbus (Ohio) Metropolitan Libraries System called "Business Resources on the Internet," the author created an "Internet Business Ready-Reference Collection." The focus client group was an urban community of public library clients. The collection consists of Internet resources that could be valuable in a small to large public library and could be used for business ready-reference. The entire project took about two hours to plan and outline; four hours to collect, evaluate, and select the business information resources; and four hours more to create a Website for the workshop.

How Many People Will be Needed to Plan, Collect, Evaluate, and Select Internet Resources, and Then to Maintain the E-library?

The number of people needed to work on the e-library will depend on the intended comprehensivenss of the e-library.

One person working with computer systems staff can do most small projects. Larger projects such as the Columbus Metropolitan Libraries System's Library Channel project require the participation of entire departments or the LII, which has 68 part-time volunteer selectors. However, even a very large project like Cyberstacks can be constructed and maintained by one person with adequate time and computer systems support.

Developing a Collection Plan for the Web-based E-Library

Constructing a Web-based e-library can be as routine as developing a print collection if you've thoughtfully made your decisions in the planning stage. A collection development plan is helpful in guiding the selection of Internet resources that will be included in the e-library. These questions will guide your collection development plan.

1. What purpose will your Web-based e-library collection serve? What subject areas will you include? For whom are you collecting Internet resources?
2. What types of Internet and other electronic resources will you link to through your e-library?
3. How will you organize the e-library? By subject? By resource type? By type of library service they might fit under?

Once your collection plan is ready, collecting the resources is basically a research task. Search for or otherwise collect the sites that seem appropriate, then evaluate whether the sites are suitable for your library clients and are of high quality, reliability, and timeliness. See Companion Website or the Web-based tutorial "Advanced Web Searching Tips and Techniques."

What Purpose Will Your Web-based E-library Collection Serve? What Subject Areas Will You Include? For Whom are You Collecting Internet Resources?

These questions are closely related. The purpose any library collection serves is contingent on the community of clients for which it is collected. The subject areas that will be included are defined by the purpose the library will serve for the intended community of clients. Every library will have their own answer to these questions.

Will your clients use the e-library for current awareness and recreational information? Research? Homework help? Business support? Legal research? How will an e-library collection benefit your clients? Most libraries will find that an e-library collection greatly extends the scope and access of their available collection. Internet resources are not always the best resource, but when smaller or isolated libraries can provide Internet access to their clients, they can often provide access to information they might not have been able to with traditional information formats. For example, in Ohio, every library regardless of size and location can have access to the full text of the Ohio Revised Code and Ohio Administrative Code, through the OPLIN Website e-library (http://oplin.lib.oh.us). Even libraries that can't afford to purchase the large multi-volume print set and updates can provide their clients with access to that information. Every library in the United States can now provide their clients with a searchable full-text and image database of patents and trademarks courtesy of the United States Patent and Trademark Office (www.uspto.gov). No longer is it necessary for everyone to pay for commercial online database access, or to purchase and maintain an expensive microform collection of patents. Granted, the USPTO patent and trademark databases do not allow the complex report options that many special and academic libraries will need (which the commercial databases provide) but for everyone else the USPTO Website is invaluable.

In what subject areas do your clients need information? Nursing? Medicine? Business? Legal issues? Literature? Computer science? Reader's advisory? Recreational information? Music? Using existing collection development plans is the most efficient way to decide. The University of Canterbury, Columbus Metropolitan Libraries, and most of the other e-library builder stories in this book used their existing plans rather than developing new ones just for Internet resource collection.

Are your clients members of the general public? Students? What age and educational level are the clients who will be using your e-library? Are you serving businesses? If so, what types? What kinds and levels of research will clients be doing? Are they graduate students, faculty, or undergraduates?

The library client population characteristics will define the scope of your e-library subject coverage, establish the complexity level of resources collected, and outline the areas of information that will be collected. Every library will need to decide individually what their clients' information needs and levels are.

What Types of Internet and Other Electronic Resources Will You Link to Through Your E-library?

A taxonomy of Internet resources adapted from Demas et al. (1995: 288) is outlined in Table 1.1. Notice how closely the types of resources on the Internet match the types of resources that we are already using in our libraries. There are both advantages and disadvantages to having these resources available through the Internet. In most cases the advantages outweigh the disadvantages as McGeachin (1998) points out:

> Internet electronic materials have the advantage of supporting new information formats and new types of interaction with users. For example, a phone directory may include the ability to see a map of the location found and give driving instructions on how to get there from almost any place in the country. Another example is the ability to look at real-time weather data with maps showing the distribution and movement of clouds, rain, wind, and temperature. Multimedia encyclopedias and handbooks can include images, audio, and video to enhance and accompany the text. Many Internet chemical materials now include the option to view and interactively rotate and examine chemical compound images. (p. 3).

Table 1.1. Taxonomy of Internet Reference Resource Types.
Adapted from Demas et al. (1995: 288)

1. Directories
2. Dictionaries
3. Abstracts, Indexes, and Table of Contents Services
4. Encyclopedias and Almanacs
5. E-Serials
6. Bibliographies and Bibliographic Databases—See Webliographies of Metasites
7. News
8. Key Primary Documents (such as Annual Reports, Law Codes, or Statistical Sources)
9. E-mail distributed (such as Listserv, Majordomo, or Listproc)
10. Usenet Newsgroups

How Will Your Organize the E-library? By Subject? By Resource Type? By Type of Library Service They Might Fit Under?

This question will always be answered differently by each library, depending on their answers to the first question of what purpose your e-library will serve. Resource organization is partially a matter of style. The simplest and probably the most accessible information structure for client access is simple broad-subject organization, organized by resource types under each subject and sub-topic umbrella heading. Or a library might want to have an organization based on their library divisions, departments, or branches; for example, periodicals department, special collections, medical library, or a particular branch library. Gerry McKiernan, Cyberstacks e-library builder, outlines a variety of different organizational structures for e-libraries in his Website "Beyond Bookmarks: Schemes for Organizing the Web" (www.public.iastate.edu/~CYBERSTACKS/CTW.htm).

Identifying and Collecting Internet Resources

The process of identifying and collecting Internet resources is similar to that of identifying and collecting print or locally-held electronic resources. One difference is that there is frequently no acquisitions process requiring financial or contractual exchanges. This section discusses the various tools on and off the Internet that can be used to identify and collect Internet resources. Examples of favorite tools will be described in the discussion. A more complete Webliography of general Internet collection tools is included in Chapter Two of this book. In general, there are several types of collection tools that you can use, including:

1. Websites which review and evaluate Internet resources: such as other e-libraries or subject collection guides/Webliographies.
2. Discussion lists and newsgroups where individual participants review and evaluate Internet resources.
3. E-journals and e-newsletters which publish reviews and evaluations of Internet resources.
4. Print books and journals which review Internet resources

Websites Which Review and Evaluate Internet Resources: Such as Other E-libraries or Subject Collection Guides/ Webliographies

The first place to look for resources to collect are in other people's e-libraries or directories of resources. This strategy is analogous to searching other libraries' catalogs, or OCLC Worldcat, RLN's Eureka, or subject bibliographies. General sites are included in the Webliography in the next chapter and specific subject sites are included with each subsequent chapter. The LII, Michigan Electronic Libraries, InfoMine, Cyberstacks, University of Canterbury, and Taft Middle School e-libraries all include annotations. The LII reviews each resource individually; initials and contact information for the reviewer are included. LII, InfoMine, and Cyberstacks are included in the "Multi-Subject Reviewed or Annotated Web Resource Directories and Electronic Library Collections" Webliography and as advanced subject search tools in the Companion Website tutorial.

Discussion Lists and Newsgroups Where Individual Participants Review and Evaluate Internet Resources

A second successful identification and collection strategy is to have each person responsible for collecting resources in a particular subject area subscribe to the core discussion lists and newsgroups related to that subject area. This strategy is analogous to asking colleagues in your library or through telephone or postal mail for their opinions of library materials.

Discussion lists and newsgroups are easy to find. Choosing which discussions and groups will be most appropriate for a given subject can be difficult. Specific groups will be recommended in subsequent chapters. There are two tools available, however, which identify the discussions and groups that are most likely to be useful for scholarly or professional research. These are *The Directory of Scholarly and Professional Electronic Conferences* (through www.arl.org/scomm/edir/) and the PHOAKS project (www.phoaks.com). *The Directory of Scholarly and Professional Electronic Conferences* is a selective directory of discussion lists, newsgroups, mailing lists, chats, and MUDs (multiuser online meeting software) which have a scholarly or professional topic. It is also published annually in print along with the *ARL Directory of Electronic Journals* (www.arl.org/scomm/edir/) as *The ARL Directory of Electronic Journals, Newsletters, and Academic Discussion Lists*. The PHOAKS project is a filtering project which looks through collections of Usenet newsgroups to find and extract messages about Internet resources—opinions are read, classified, and tallied automatically. Their motto is "People Helping One Another Know Stuff."

The Net-Happenings and NetInLib-Announce Internet distribution lists exist entirely for the purpose of reviewing and discussing Internet resources and Internet-related events.

E-journals and E-newsletters Which Publish Reviews and Evaluations of Internet Resources

This strategy is analogous to using CHOICE reviews, *Library Journal,* or other sources of book reviews. Many print journals and newsletters are now publishing electronic versions on the Web. These are discussed under the "Print books and journals . . . " section below. There are hundreds of e-journals that publish reviews of Internet resources that are published only on the Web or distributed through e-mail. These can sometimes be difficult to identify. Ann Okerson and James J. O'Donnell, however, moderate a distribution list called NewJour which distributes e-mail announcements of new electronic journals and newsletters to subscribers.

The Association of Research Libraries (ARL) publishes an annual directory of online journals and newsletters based on the NewJour distributions. The title is the *ARL Directory of Electronic Journals, Newsletters, and Academic Discussion Lists.*

Subscribers can get access to a searchable database version of this directory as well as the searchable NewJour archives (http://gort.ucsd.edu/newjour/). As of this writing the current edition is the seventh, published in January 1998, and the 1999 eighth edition is in production. One particularly useful Internet e-newsletter is *The Scout Report* (http://scout.cs.wisc.edu/index.html). *The Scout Report* is published by the Internet Scout Project. Susan Calcari is the Internet Scout Project director. The Internet Scout Project team collects and reviews Internet resources and publishes the reviews in a weekly e-newsletter that is distributed through e-mail as well as published on their Website. There are five different versions of *The Scout Report* available for free subscription: SCOUT-REPORT, *The Scout Report*; SCOUT-REPORT-HTML, *The Scout Report HTML* version; SRBUSECON, *The Scout Report for Business and Economics*; SRSCIENG, *The Scout Report for Science and Engineering*; and SRSOCSCI, *The Scout Report for Social Sciences* (see http://scout18.cs.wisc.edu/cgi-bin/lwgate/listsavail.html). Another good example is the *Internet Tourbus* e-newsletter published on Tuesdays and Thursdays by Patrick Douglas Crispen and Bob Rankin. The *Internet Tourbus* is a "virtual tour of the best of the Internet, delivered by e-mail . . . " (www.tourbus.com).

Print Books and Journals Which Review Internet Resources

In the last few years dozens of books have been published that are essentially annotated Webliographies of Internet resources. Because print sources are quickly out of date, only the most recent publications which cover general reference sources or collection development tools will be mentioned here; additional titles will be included in each of the subsequent subject-oriented chapters.

The Information Specialists Guide to Searching & Researching on the Internet & the World Wide Web (1998) by Ackerman and Hartman is an outstanding source. It not only identifies many of the same Internet collection development tools which are in this book's Webliographies, it also annotates and evaluates them as search tools. *Reference Sources on the Internet : Off the Shelf and Onto the Web* (1997) edited by Karen R. Diaz is a collection of articles focused on the collection of Internet reference sources in different subject areas. Although some of the sources mentioned are already moved, replaced, or defunct, the strategies for Internet resource collection planning are still valid. *Reference and Collection Development on the Internet: A How-To-Do-It Manual* (1996) by Elizabeth Thomsen is interesting in that it was the first book of its type. At this writing, most of the practical collection strategies discussed in Thomsen's book are obsolete (FTP, WAIS, Gopher), but the discussion of the raison d'etre for electronic reference collections remains a stimulating and useful one.

Many journals in library science as well as other subject areas are now carrying regular columns or special issues which review a variety of Internet resources. Many of these print journals are archiving their Web resource reviews—and other selected portions of the parent publication—for free access on the Web. In the library profession, *Choice: Current Reviews for Academic Libraries* has been a standard collection development tool for all materials. *Choice* has been carrying Internet resource reviews for some time and recently began issuing special supplements which focus on reviews of Web resources. The reviews from previous years are archived on their Website (http://ala8.ala.org/acrl/choice/other.html). *Booklist* also publishes a "Reference on the Web" review section in each issue and archives the previous year's reviewed sites on their Website (http://ala8.ala.org/booklist). *College and Research Libraries, College and Research Libraries News, American Libraries, Library Journal,* and others, have also been publishing articles which evaluate and describe Internet resources. One of the most useful and interesting is the *American Libraries* "Internet Librarian" column. Columnist Karen Schneider features discussions of different valuable, controversial, or otherwise interesting aspects of librarians' interactions with the Internet. The "Internet Librarian" columns and other articles from the *American Libraries* journal are available at the *American Libraries Online* Website (http://ala8.ala.org/alonline). *College and Research Libraries News* publishes a special Internet version called *College and Research Libraries News* Net on their Website (www.ala.org/acrl/c&rlnew2.html). Each issue features reviews of Internet resources in some subject area.

Information Evaluation Criteria and Practical Application of Information Evaluation Criteria to Internet Information

We all know the basics of information evaluation. The real key is to know how to find the information that we need in order to successfully evaluate Internet resources. We also may need to teach our clients about Internet information evaluation. In fact, some authors suggest that our role vis-à-vis Internet information should be one of evaluating and endorsing particular sites (Sowards, 1998)

This section will discuss general evaluative criteria, but more importantly it will discuss the specific places to look for the information that will allow you to evaluate an Internet resource based on that evaluative criteria.

A Webliography of additional articles and workshops on evaluating Internet information is provided in the next chapter. A book by Cooke (1999), *Neal-Schuman Authoritative Guide to Evaluating Information on the Internet* has just been published. Prepublication information indicates that this will be a very useful tool for e-library resource evaluators and selectors.

There are three kinds of knowledge we need to have or acquire to enable evaluation of Internet information:

1. Awareness of the nature of Internet information: Stuff and Good Stuff on the Internet.
2. Awareness and understanding of basic problems with information obtained from the Internet.
3. How to acquire the information needed to determine the source, authority, accuracy, timeliness, purpose, security, and privacy of Internet information.

The Three Kinds of Knowledge Necessary to Evaluate Internet Information

1. Nature—Awareness of the nature of Internet information: Stuff and Good Stuff on the Internet
2. Problems—Awareness and understanding of basic problems with information obtained from the Internet.
3. Source Determination—How to acquire the information needed to determine the source. It is useful to remember the mnemonic PAST: purpose and privacy; authority and accuracy; source and security; and timeliness.

Awareness of the Nature of Internet Information: Stuff and Good Stuff on the Internet

In order to apply information evaluation criteria to Internet information, it is necessary to understand the term "Internet information." An explanation that has been useful in teaching Internet information evaluation workshops has been the concept of "stuff" and "good stuff." Most information on the Internet is just "stuff." "Good stuff" is any of the information on the Internet that is relevant to the information needs of your client, and meets basic quality-of-information standards.

Stuff on the Internet

In general, "stuff" on the Internet can be found on personal private Web pages where people are expressing their opinions, ideas, and tastes, and providing their personal information. Commercial advertising pages are often just simple statements of a commercial entity's existence. People just talking about recreational or personal matters using discussion lists or newsgroups (MUDs, IRC, or Web Chat, for example) also make up a great deal of the "stuff" on the Internet. It is important to keep in mind that a great deal of information on the Internet and Web is actually the transcripts—called archives—from discussion groups, newsgroups, and chats.

Good Stuff on the Internet

An outline of the source types of "stuff" and "good stuff" on the Internet is reproduced in Tables 1.2 and 1.3. Notice that there are many overlaps in information source types. The reality is that one person's "stuff" might be another person's "good stuff." Personal pages and commercial pages can offer quality, useful content, as can discussion lists, newsgroups, and chats and their archives on the Web. Internet information types have their analogies in print and other media: a program on TV can be something like "Entertainment Tonight," or "The News Hour with Jim Lehrer"; a newspaper might be *The New York Times* or the *National Enquirer*; a radio program might be *Diane Rehm* or *Don Imus*.

Personal private Web pages might only contain information about the opinions and personal life of an individual or they might contain valuable educational or recreation information. Valuable, that is, for someone who is interested and needs the information they provide. For example, most of the good quilting pages are provided by quilters to share with other quilters on personal private Web pages. Some of the best music, books, and movie reviews can also be found on personal private Web pages. Commercial pages may be simple advertisements with no useful content, or they might provide access to product catalogs, technical support information, or even e-commerce. Organizational pages might provide information for recreational or educational

---

Table 1.2. Stuff on the Internet

Personal Private Web Pages

Commercial Advertising Pages

Organizational Pages with a Recreational or Political Intent

Personal Web Pages that Offer Valuable Educational Information

Discussion Lists and Newsgroups with Recreational or Political Intent

(MUDS, IRC, or Web Chat for example) or People Just Talking

---

interests that is useful or interesting for one client but not for another. Government Web pages generally provide information that is as good as any other format in which the government provides information.

The Internet information "stuff" and "good stuff" concepts are useful as a loose model for clarifying the problem of classifying Internet information. These concepts cannot help directly in solving the problems of evaluating Internet resources as sources of information. This is because one person's "good stuff" is just another person's "stuff" or even another person's "bad stuff." It is also simply not possible to evaluate information based solely on the type of Website or the domain address of the information provider (there is a possible exception in that .gov sites are highly likely to provide accurate, timely, and potentially useful information). There are other factors that must be explored before evaluative judgements can be made.

Table 1.3. Good Stuff on the Internet

Personal Web Pages that Offer Valuable Educational Information

Commercial Pages that Offer Product Support, Directory Services, Tutorials, or Other Valuable Services

Government Pages that Provide Government Collected Information

Educational Pages from Universities, Colleges, Schools, Museums, and Other Organizations with Educational Missions.

Discussion Lists and Newsgroups with Education, Research, or Professional Intent

MUDS, IRC, or Web Chat or People Just Talking About Matters of Interest

---

Awareness and Understanding of Basic Problems with Information Obtained from the Internet

Some basic problems with information obtained from the Internet, or just about anywhere else for that matter, are listed below in order of their observed frequency on the Web:

1. Typos
2. Factual Errors (Accidental or Deliberate)
3. Opinion Stated as Fact
4. Out-of-Date Information
5. Bias
6. Deliberate Fraud

Typos

The information provided on the Internet comes from many sources. Typos are one of the most prevalent problems, because **anyone** can publish information on the Internet and there are often no editors or publishing agencies to review the information. Typos are probably most frequently caused by two factors: inaccurate typing because of the informality of the medium and language ignorance.

There is one factor that is unique to the Internet: Much information on the Internet was originally part of a conversation. Discussion list, newsgroups, MOO, and chat are text based but they are really more akin to speech than to publications. The difference between speech and published information is primarily formality of the language. The Internet was described by a special three-judge panel which heard the first *ACLU vs. Reno* trial (Communications Decency Act) as an enormous "world-wide conversation" (ACLU Website: court brief at www.aclu.org/court/renovaclu.html; judges decision at www.aclu.org/court/cdadec.html). Some parts of that world-wide conversation are very literate and very authoritative, and others are not.

Factual Errors (Accidental or Deliberate)

These usually happen because people simply are not checking, or sometimes are making up information. During an Internet searching workshop I taught in 1993, the only answer we could find on the Internet to the question "What was the year of the first Thanksgiving?" was 1676. According to the *Information Please: Online Dictionary, Internet Encyclopedia, & Almanac Reference* (www.infoplease.com), the actual year of the first Thanksgiving is either 1621, 1789, or 1863 depending on whether you mean the first celebration or the year that it was declared a holiday by George Washington or Abraham Lincoln. The answer we found in 1993—at a site which no longer exists—was supplied by a sixth grader at a suburban Chicago school. This example is not meant to imply that sixth graders are always a source of inaccurate information. A sixth grader might publish accurate information if they acquire the facts from an authoritative source (teacher) and or document their source (encyclopedia, almanac or Website).

Opinion Stated as Fact

This problem is very prevalent on the Internet. Do you question the veracity of something *just* because of who published it? Where the Internet is concerned, yes, you must question the veracity of information based on who said it. You have to ask "Did the person/doctor/sixth grader have training or do research that gives them the authority to provide the information? Can that person provide documentation/proof that what they say is accurate? What type of information is provided online to make these determinations? In the next section we'll discuss strategies for answering these questions about Internet information. We do the same kinds of evaluation when we work with print resources. Looking at the author of an article and finding their sources, research, training, and background before believing what they say or write. Some of the evaluation with print resources in libraries is already done at the stage of making the acquisitions decision. Decisions are made during the acquisitions process such as if a particular publisher accepted and published a book or journal then it must by association be of good quality. Internet research evaluation is more difficult. It involves more primary research than we are used to doing.

Out-of-date Information

This kind of problem is one that is surprising, considering how easy it is to update Web pages and other Internet information sources. But people don't always have the time or ability to update information or to take it offline when it is out of date. For example, student project Websites might remain online long after the project is finished and the student graduates. Another problem is that so much information on the Internet is actually archives of discussion lists and newsgroups. It is important to check the dates of the individual postings in such archives.

Bias

Bias is a bigger problem with all source of information than many people realize. There are many sites on the Internet—as well as every other publication medium—where information is provided with a slant in order to try to influence people to think about something in a particular way. An illustrative example is the "Jefferson Party" Website (www.alaska.net/~winter/). They express beliefs such as "The true constitution of the United States of America, known as the Constitution of the United States, has been hidden from the People of the United States of America." The "Jefferson Party" page could be considered good stuff for researchers studying political activism and extremism in the U.S or for someone who concurred with the beliefs expressed on that page.

Election campaign information is always biased. For that matter so is advertising information. Probably every piece of information reflects bias of some kind. The degree, type of, and reason for bias must be considered in evaluating information.

Deliberate Fraud

This is rare but does happen. The worst example I could find on the Web was an incident in 1996 when a Massachusetts woman advertised on her Web page that if you bought her patent medicine you would be "HIV Negative in Six Weeks!" She sold it over the Web and many people were victimized. This was discussed in "AIDS-Related Quackery and Fraud" by Stephen Barrett, M.D. on the Quackwatch Website (www.quackwatch.com).

We've discussed "stuff" and "good stuff" but there is also "bad stuff" on the Internet. "Bad stuff" is anything that you, your clients, or your community consider criminal, evil, or otherwise unacceptable. For example, for some people, racist, sexist, hate-speech, anti-government, historical-revisionist, or pornography sites are "bad stuff." For some sociology, political-science, or psychology researchers—especially where libraries, as opposed to private individuals, are concerned—these sites can be "good stuff" as sources for sociological, political, or economic research.

How to Acquire the Information Needed to Determine the Source, Authority, Accuracy, Timeliness, Purpose, Security, and Privacy of Internet Information

Quality of information varies on the Internet, because anyone can publish information without review. In general, use the same criteria used to judge information from print or other media.

Evaluation criteria for Internet information can be reduced to five key concepts:

1. Authority of the Information Source
2. Accuracy of the Information
3. Timeliness of the Information in Reference to the Information Type and the Needs of the Client
4. Security of the Information: Is the Site Liable to be Hacked and Information Altered? Does the Site Request Clients to Submit Personal or Financial Information?
5. Privacy of the Client When Using the Information

Table 1.4. Accuracy and Timeliness of Internet Information —Key Questions

1. Who provided the information? What is their reputation as an Information Provider?
2. Does the information provider have the authority or expertise to provide information on that topic?
3. What is the purpose for which the information is being provided?
4. Is the information provided for current information or historical purposes?
5. Is the resource affected by currency or lack of currency?
6. When was the last update of the information?

Or simpler still:

The underlying concept is reputation. What do you know and what have you learned to expect from a person or organization? Reputation is based on what we know about the authority of the information source and the purpose for which the information is provided. Table 1.4 outlines the key questions that should be asked about information of any kind. Table 1.5 outlines the strategies for finding the answers to these questions about Internet information. In the discussion below these questions and strategies are clustered together because the strategies for finding the answers to the questions are similar or even the same.

Who provided the information? What is their reputation as an information provider? Does the information provider have the authority or expertise to provide information on that topic? What is the purpose for which the information is being provided? Is the information provided for current information or historical purposes? Does currency or lack of currency affect the quality of the information? When was the last update of the information?

One problem with the Internet is that many information providers haven't had time to establish a reputation. The Internet has only been available for the general public in the United States since around 1992. Reputation requires time and exposure to public opinion. Finding out who the information provider is and their authority is usually possible, as is finding out the purpose for which the information is provided and whether or not it is current. If you cannot at least find out who provided the information, however, then you cannot use it in a library, teaching, or research environment. All of us have been trained to cite a source when we answer a question. For example, earlier in this chapter I said: "According to the *Information Please: Online Dictionary, Internet Encyclopedia, & Almanac Reference* (www.infoplease.com), the actual year of the first Thanksgiving is either 1621, 1789, or 1863 depend-

---

**Table 1.5. Accuracy and Timeliness of Internet Information
—How to Find the Answers**

1. Read through Web pages associated with the site.
2. View the "Document Info" or "Page Info" of Web pages to look for author identification and/or publication date.
3. View the HTML "Page Source" or "Document Source" of Web pages to look for author identification and/or publication date.
4. If you are a subject expert, use your own judgement, otherwise ask a subject expert to review the information.
5. Find reviews of Internet resources by qualified reviewers or use selective subject directory/electronic library collections to identify resources.
6. E-mail the person or organization identified as responsible and ask them to answer the questions.
7. If you can't find an e-mail address on the page or in the HTML source information, then try e-mailing: hostmaster @ <the base domain from the URL> or postmaster@<the base URL> where <the base domain from the URL> is the first part of the URL minus the "WWW" part. For example, if you wanted to find the contact for www.kovacs.com/eval.html and don't see an e-mail address on it, then try sending e-mail to: hostmaster@www.kovacs.com or to postmaster@kovacs.com.
8. On newsgroups and discussion lists ask the speaker to qualify themselves.
9. Search offline or in commercial databases to identify the authority of an Internet Information Provider.

---

ing on whether you mean the first celebration or the year that it was declared a holiday by George Washington or Abraham Lincoln."

In order to find that answer, I first read through Web pages associated with the site. In this case I clicked on the "Company" link at the bottom of the page and found that the publisher of this Website is the same company that publishes the classic *Information Please Almanac* and others. They have a 50 year history behind them. Furthermore, they provided contact information so I can talk to a person. This is a best case example. Some Websites do not provide such easy access to the information provider's identification information. So the first thing you need to do is read through the Website to find the answers to all of the evaluative questions. If still you don't find attribution information, but the information is valuable enough or you have reason to believe that the attribution information was left out inadvertently, here are some other strategies:

- View the "Document Info" or "Page Info" of Web pages to look for author identification and/or publication date.

Use your Web browser's "View" menu option and choose "Page Info" or "Document Info" depending on what version of browser you have. This option shows information about publication dates and page authors when that information has been provided by an HTML editor or coded in by the author.

- View the HTML "Page Source" or "Document Source" of Web pages to look for author identification and/or publication date.

Use your Web browser's "View" menu option and choose "Page Source" or "Document Source" depending on what version of browser you have. You will be looking at the raw HTML of the page. Some HTML editing software will automatically insert the author information provided by the page author's operating system. If so, the author name will appear in the <Meta> tag field. For example, if you look at the "Page Source" for www.kovacs.com, you will see: <meta name="Author" content="Diane K. Kovacs">.

- If you are a subject expert, use your own judgement, otherwise ask a subject expert to review the information.

- Find reviews of Internet resources by qualified reviewers or use selective subject directory/electronic library collections to identify resources.

Some good review sources are provided in the Webliographies.

In order to establish the authority of an Internet information provider, the first step is to again read through the Website to find out the education, experience, research background, or other authority which the information provider says they have. If the authority information is not on the Website or if the information is critical, e-mail the person or organization identified as responsible and ask them to answer the questions about their education, experience, research background, etc. There should be an e-mail address or other contact information on a well-designed Web page. Lack of contact information may also indicate that no one is willing to take responsibility for the content of the Web page. If you cannot find contact information on the Web page or in the HTML source—and if the content is valuable enough or you have reason to believe that contact information was left off inadvertently—then try e-mailing: hostmaster@<the base domain from the URL> or postmaster@<the base URL> where <the base domain from the URL> is the first part of the URL minus the "WWW" part. For example, if you wanted to find the contact for www.kovacs.com/eval.html and don't see an e-mail address on it, then try sending e-mail to: hostmaster@www.kovacs.com or to postmaster@kovacs.com. When you are participating in or reading the archives of discussion lists and newsgroups, ask the writer to qualify themselves. There is nothing wrong with doing a search offline or in commercial data-

---

Table 1.6. Security and Privacy of Internet Information —Key Questions

1. Is security important in interacting with a given Internet information source? Is a site liable to be hacked and information altered? Will personal or financial information be requested from clients?
2. Is privacy of information seeking behavior an important factor for you or your clients?
3. How can you protect your security and privacy on the Internet?

---

bases to verify or validate the authority of an Internet information provider. You can search to see if they've published anything else in the area in print or other media.

Verifying the security and privacy of Internet information

The key questions to ask in order to verify security and privacy of Internet information are outlined in Table 1.6; the answers and strategies are outlined in Table 1.7.

The most important question is: Is security important in interacting with a given Internet information source? If the Website is not asking for personal or financial information then the client's security is not an issue. However, the second question, regarding whether a site is liable to be hacked and information altered, might still be important.

If security of the personal or financial information is important, then use your Web browser functions to verify security of a Web page. In Netscape, the padlock in the lower left corner will close when you enter a secure page. In Internet Explorer and Netscape use the "View" then "Page Info" or "Document Info" option to check for security status. You can set most browsers to warn you when you are entering or leaving a secure page.

Table 1.7. Security of Internet Information—Some Answers

1. Use your Web browser functions to verify security of a Web page. On a Netscape page, the padlock in the lower left corner will close when you enter a secure page. In Internet Explorer and Netscape use the "View" then "Page Info" or "Document Info" option to check for security status. You can set most browsers to warn you when you are entering or leaving a secure page.
2. Privacy of Internet Information—There is no privacy on the Internet: When you connect to a Web page you can be counted and your movements through the site tracked.

Secure Web servers ensure that only the intended recipient of your information can receive and use it. This is analogous to your calling an 800 number and ordering from a catalog. Putting your information into a form on an unsecure Web page is analogous to giving out your credit card information over a cell phone or to someone who called you and solicited the information from you.

There is a fascinating piece on computer hacking and Websites on the CNN Website at http://cnn.com/TECH/specials/hackers/. Hackers have altered the information stored on a number of important Websites including the CIA Website. Hackers can get into most standard Web servers unless great care is taken to configure and maintain server security. True information security requires excellent server security and a reliable certification and authentication system between the suppliers of the information and the Web server. This helps to ensure that only individuals authorized by the information provider may add or change information on the Website.

If privacy of information-seeking behavior is an important factor for you or your clients, then the Internet might not be a good choice for you. There is no privacy on the Internet. When you connect to a Web page you can be counted and your movements through the site tracked. For example, look at Metacrawler's MetaSpy site (www.metacrawler.com/perl/metaspy) to peek at what other people are searching for using the Metacrawler Search Engine. Also look at Privacy.Net (http://privacy.net/) or Who Am I? (www.mall-net.com/cgibin/whoami.cgi?src=webcons). These latter two Websites are tools to test the privacy or lack thereof provided by your particular connection to the Internet. The best strategy to ensure privacy is to use an Internet-connected computer available to the public at a library or Internet cafe. Then the only thing the Website owners can discover about you is where you connected from and that someone there is interested in their site.

Another issue related to security and privacy is the use of "cookies" by Websites to record your activities and to store information like logins and passwords for your personal connections to their site. A "cookie" is described at Netscape's Website (http://home.netscape.com/newsref/std/cookie_spec.html) in the following terms:

> This simple mechanism provides a powerful new tool which enables a host of new types of applications to be written for web-based environments. Shopping applications can now store information about the currently selected items, for fee services can send back registration information and free the client from retyping a user-id on next connection, sites can store per-user preferences on the client, and have the client supply those preferences every time that site is connected to.

Cookies are the Internet equivalent of the "frequent shopper card." In exchange for marketing information and a certain loss of privacy, the client may receive benefits such as free and simple access to a site. If cookie-based registrations or logins are used at a public Internet terminal there is a danger that the next client using that terminal will be able to access the private information of other clients.

Selection Criteria for Internet Resources

Electronic resources, Internet, or other electronic formats have some special considerations. Does the library have computer resources to provide access to the resource? Is the search system easily used? Is the search system adequate to locate information in the database? Can the database be networked or be used with a locally developed end-user interface? What is the total cost of implementation? Not every electronic version of an information product is superior to the print version. The *Oxford English Dictionary*, for example, is much easier to search by simply opening the books and looking up the words than using the CD-ROM, although the CD-ROM does provide complex search and report features.

Table 1.8. Access Criteria for Internet Resources

Selection Adapted from Caywood (1996) (www6.pilot.infi.net/~carolyn/criteria.html)

Is the site still useable with an ASCII browser like Lynx, or with software for people with disabilities?

Is it written in standard HTML, or have proprietary extensions been used?

Does it use standard multimedia formats?

Must you download software to use it?

Do parts of it take too long to load?

Is it usually possible to reach the site, or is it overloaded?

Is it stable, or has the URL changed?

Is the URL stated in the text of the Web page?

Does the site use the words the average person would try in a search engine?

Is it open to everyone on the Internet, or do parts require membership and/or fees?

If there is a charge, can the library pay it on a subscription basis for multiple access points?

Are any rules for use stated up front?

Table 1.9. Design Criteria for Internet Resources

Selection Adapted from Caywood (1996) (www6.pilot.infi.net/~carolyn/criteria.html)

Are the individual Web pages concise, or do you have to heavily scroll?

Do essential instructions appear before links and interactive portions?

Do all the parts work?

Is using the site intuitive, or are parts likely to be misunderstood?

Can you find your way around and easily locate a particular page from any other page?

Is it obvious when you move to a new site, or does an outside link appear internal?

Is the structure stable, or do features disappear between visits?

Does it look and feel friendly?

Are backgrounds or other visual elements distracting or cluttered?

Is it conceptually exciting? Does it do more than can be done with print?

If Java or ActiveX, extensions like frames, or plug-ins are employed, do they actually improve the site? How will they affect users with older browsers?

In her Web-published article "Library Selection Criteria for WWW Resources" Caywood (1996) (www6.pilot.infi.net/~carolyn/criteria.html) shares a great listing of criteria for assessing the value of Websites for library clients. The criteria are organized under three main concepts: access, design, and content. These are outlined and edited for currency and compatibility with the structure of this chapter in Tables 1.8, 1.9 and 1.10.

McGeachin (1998) also identifies the key issues that are unique to selection of Internet resources. These are similar to those identified by Caywood but he adds concerns about long-term archiving of information and licensing of access to information on the Internet. Even fee-based licensed access to information can be justified if funding is available, because:

> When a library, university system, or consortium, acquires a web-based product, it essentially provides multiple copies since the product can be widely distributed to a very large client base. If the system components are spread over a large geographical area, this can provide much easier remote access to the materials. Increasing interest in distance education seems to be a trend at many educational institutions, and as a result, the need to supply library materials to distant locations is growing. Providing Internet access to full text materials for remote users is one solution to this service issue. (p. 2).

Table 1.10. Content Criteria for Internet Resources

Selection Adapted from Caywood (1996) (www6.pilot.infi.net/~carolyn/criteria.html)

Are the scope and limits clearly stated? Is the title informative? Does the content fit the stated scope?

Does the content meet the standards for accuracy, authority, timeliness, security, and privacy tested for during the evaluation process?

Is the content unique, or readily available elsewhere? Has copyright been respected?

Does the content meet information needs of the client community you are collecting resources for?

Are headings clear and descriptive, or do they use jargon unknown to the average user?

Is text well-written with acceptable grammar and spelling? What is the quality of multimedia files?

Is the content organized by the needs of the user, or does it reflect an internal hierarchy?

If there is advertising, what is its relevance and proportion to the rest of the site?

Are there reviews of the site? How many other sites link to this one?

Selection criteria for any kind of information resource are derived from the answers arrived at during the collection planning process. Therefore, the core criteria will always be:

1. Does the resource meet some information need of the e-library's intended clients?
2. Does the resource provide the information at a level and language suitable to the age, educational background, and subject interests of the e-library's intended clients?
3. Does the resource provide information in a form that you want to include in your e-library (for example, encyclopedias, directories, e-serials, or e-commerce facilities)?

Other selection criteria specific to Internet resources are:

4. Access and Design
   Will the e-library's intended clients have the computer equipment and software needed to use the resource? Does the resource allow for access

by disabled individuals who may need to use text-to-voice software or other enabling tools? Does the resource display in the Web browser within a reasonable amount of time over the expected mode of access?

Bobby (www.cast.org/bobby) is a tool that allows you to submit the URL of a Web page and evaluates its accessibility to everyone regardless of physical handicaps. It is also an HTML compatibility checker. According to the Bobby site documentation, "Bobby also analyzes Web pages for compatibility with various browsers. Analysis is based on documentation from browser vendors when available."

5. Archiving
   Will the information provider provide 'back issues' or archives of the resource? Will you need to make arrangements to store such information locally if needed? This is especially important in the case of e-serials or current information that will become valuable historical information over time. Most scientific research information will require some kind of archiving arrangements be made. The information may be archived in print publications, backed up to CD-ROM, magnetic tape or other electronic storage media, or simply kept available on the Web for an indeterminate period as long as researchers are assured that it will be archived and available in the future. Obviously, researchers may prefer that it be archived in some format that is easily accessible.

6. Cost/Licensing/User Access Control
   Some Internet accessible resources are fee-based. If that is the case, as with, for example, the Encyclopedia Britannica online, consideration will need to be made for not only the cost of the resource, but any licensing arrangements or user access control that must be exercised. For instance, will the resource only be accessible by users from within the library's domain, or can any library user from any location access the resource by using a login and password or library card number?

The Ready Reference Internet reference core collection included in Chapter Two was compiled with these criteria in mind. The intended client group is, very broadly, any English-speaking person who might want ready-reference type information. The access and design of all these core Internet reference sources are based on standards of simplicity and international Internet Web browser compatibility, with no special software required for access. Most of them are free of direct cost—except for the cost of Internet access. Some fee-based services are in addition to the free services. Archiving of most critical information at these sites is assured by the publishers who provided the information in both print and other electronic storage media.

Some General Considerations for Constructing, Organizing, and Maintaining the Web-based E-library

The creation of a Web page with links and annotations for collected Internet information resources is very simple; all that is required is a basic knowledge of HTML and an editor. There are many HTML editors available, but they all require knowledge of HTML to a greater or lesser degree in order to be used effectively, which is not to say that you couldn't cobble something together with them even if you knew nothing of HTML. The Companion Website contains a tutorial for Web page and Website creation with HTML and Netscape Composer. If you want something more complex, such as putting your e-library collection into a Web-accessible database program, you'll need to work with a computer programmer. The LII and the OPLIN (one of the e-library builder stories in Chapter 3) Website e-libraries, for example, are published in Web-accessible databases. You may also choose to make your e-library available on a standalone computer or internal LAN or Intranet (intra-organizational TCP/IP network). The Library Channel for example is only available on the library's systemwide LAN.

Maintenance of your e-library requires regular checking of links to make sure they are current and working. There is software to assist you with this type of maintenance. This software is frequently reviewed on the Web4lib discussion list. Search the Web4lib archives at http://sunsite.berkeley.edu/Web4Lib/archive.html to find link-checking software recommended by other librarians with e-library set-ups similar to yours.

Maintaining the Web-based e-library will also include ongoing collection and incorporation of new resources. Mainstreaming ongoing selection of Internet resources into the collection development responsibilities of each staff member is another consideration. Staff members will need to be trained to use the Internet effectively (learning evaluation and searching skills). The computers they use during the collection process should provide adequate memory, Internet connection speed, and current Web browser and plug-in software to make evaluative selections of, for example, multimedia and high graphics resources. Staff members need to be made aware of selection strategies defined for each library, and need to be able to communicate with each other regarding resource selections. Someone should coordinate all collection and selection efforts to avoid duplication.

Print and Electronic Publications Cited or Consulted in Chapter One

Ackerman, E. and Hartman, K. 1998. *The Information Specialists Guide to Searching & Researching on the Internet & the World Wide Web.* Wilsonville, OR: ABF Content.

Caywood, C. 1996. "Library Selection Criteria for WWW Resources. (www6.pilot.infi.net/~carolyn/criteria.html).

Cooke, A. 1999. *Neal-Schuman Authoritative Guide to Evaluating Information on the Internet.* New York: Neal-Schuman.

Coutts, M. M. 1998. "Collecting for the Researcher in an Electronic Environment," *Library Review.* 47, no 5/6: 282–289.

Demas, S. G. 1994. "Collection Development for the Electronic Library: A Conceptual and Organizational Model." *Library Hi Tech.* 12, no 3: 71–80.

Demas, S. G., McDonald, P., and Lawrence, G. 1995. "The Internet and Collection Development: Mainstreaming Selection of Internet Resources." *Library Resources and Technical Services.* 39, no 3: 275–290.

Diaz, K. R., Ed. 1997. *Reference Sources on the Internet : Off the Shelf and Onto the Web.* New York: Haworth Press.

Fedunok, S. 1997. "Hammurabi and the Electronic Age: Documenting Electronic Collection Decisions." *RQ.* 36, no 1: 86–90.

Kopp, J. J. 1997. "The Politics of a Virtual Collection." *Collection Management.* 22, no 1–2: 81–100.

Kuny, T. and Cleveland G. 1998. "The Digital Library: Myths and Challenges." *IFLA Journal.* 24, no 2: 107–113.

McGeachin, R. B. 1998. "Selection Criteria for Web-Based Resources in a Science and Technology Library Collection." *Issues in Science and Technology Librarianship.* (www.library.ucsb.edu/istl/98-spring/article2.html)

Morville, P. S. and Wickhorst, S. J. 1996. "Building Subject-Specific Guides to Internet Resources." *Internet Research: Electronic Networking Applications and Policy.* 6, no 4: 27–32.

Norman, O. G. 1997. "The Impact of Electronic Information Sources on Collection Development: A Survey of Current Practice," *Library Hi Tech.* 15, nos 1–2: 123–132.

Piontek, S. and Garlock, K. 1995. "Creating a World Wide Web Resource Collection." *Collection Building.* 14, no 1: 12–18.

Rioux, M. 1997. Hunting and Gathering in Cyberspace: Finding and Selecting Web Resources for the Library's Virtual Collection. In *Pioneering New Serials Frontiers: From Petroglyphs to Cyberserials.* Binghamton, NY: Haworth Press.

Rosenfeld, L. 1998. *Information Architecture for the World Wide Web.* Sebastopol, CA: O'Reilly and Associates, Inc.

Rosenfeld, L. Janes, J., and Vander Kolk, M. 1995. *The Internet Compendium*. New York: Neal-Schuman.

Sowards, S. W. 1998. "A Typology for Ready Reference Websites in Libraries."*First Monday*. 1, no 14. (www.firstmonday.dk/).

Stielow, F. Ed. 1999. *Creating a Virtual Library: A How-To-Do-It Manual for Integrating Information Resources on the Web*. New York: Neal-Schuman.

Tennant, R. 1998. "The Art and Science of Digital Bibliography." *Library Journal*. 123, no 17: 28–29.

Thomsen, E. 1996. *Reference and Collection Development on the Internet: A How-To-Do-It Manual for Librarians*. New York: Neal-Schuman.

Yochelson, A., Ammen, C., Guidas, J., Harvey, S., Larson, C., and McGinnis, M. 1997. "Collection Development and the Internet: A Brief Handbook for Recommending Officers in the Humanities and Social Sciences Division at the Library of Congress." (http://lcweb.loc.gov/acq/colldev/handbook.html).

Websites Cited in Chapter One (some of these are also listed with annotations in the Webliographies)

ACLU Website: Court Brief at www.aclu.org/court/renovaclu.html. Judges' decision at www.aclu.org/court/cdadec.html.

American Libraries Online Website (http://ala8.ala.org/alonline/).

Bobby (www.cast.org/bobby).

Booklist (http://ala8.ala.org/booklist/.).

Choice: Current Reviews for Academic Libraries (www.ala.org/acrl/choice/).

Collection Development Training for Arizona Public Libraries (www.dlapr.lib.az.us/cdt/index.htm).

College and Research Libraries News Net (www.ala.org/acrl/c&rlnew2.html).

Directory of Scholarly and Professional Electronic Conferences (through www.arl.org/scomm/edir/).

Internet Tourbus (www.tourbus.com).

Jefferson Party Website (www.alaska.net/~winter).

MetaCrawler's MetaSpy (www.metacrawler.com/perl/metaspy).

Netscape's Website Cookie description (http://home.netscape.com/newsref/std/cookie_spec.html).

PHOAKS project (www.phoaks.com).

Privacy. Net (http://Privacy.net/).

Quackwatch. "AIDS-Related Quackery and Fraud." (www.quackwatch.com).

Who Am I? (www.mall-net.com/cgibin/whoami.cgi?src=webcons).

2
Collecting Web-based Core Ready-reference Resources

The Core Internet Ready-reference Collection

Sowards (1998) defines the Ready-reference E-library as:

A "reference Website" is an HTML-based page (or system of pages) that provides potentially useful information by assembling hot links to online tools (some sites also include citations to paper tools). Because Website designers must assume that remote users will be working without direct human assistance or the opportunity to discuss subtle nuances, these sites emphasize factual material: reference information that addresses basic questions of the sort known to librarians as "ready reference" questions. (p. 2).

When you go into a new library as a library staff member—and sometimes as a library client—what are the first things you look for? You look for the core reference tools that you will need to assist clients or to answer your own research questions.

In May 1998, and again in May 1999, I posted the questions reproduced in Figure 2.1 and Figure 2.2 to Publib and to Libref-L. I posted the results back to both discussion lists on June 15, 1999 and reproduce them here in Figure 2.3. The results for each subject area will be discussed where appropriate in the subsequent chapters. The clear results for the core ready-reference tools, both print and electronic, make an excellent guide for Internet ready-reference tool selection. In other words, if you can find Internet ready-reference tools that are similar to the core ready-reference tools in print and other electronic forms you have the framework for a great Web-based core ready-reference collection. The top seven ready-reference tools that Publib and Libref-l subscribers can't live without, as well as the other essential ready-reference print, CD-ROM, and online reference tools are listed in Figure 2.3

Figure 2.1. May 6, 1998 Question Posted to Libref-L and Publib

Core Reference Tools?
Diane K. Kovacs (diane@kovacs.com)
Wed, 6 May 1998 19:13:58 -0700 (PDT)

Dear Publib Folks,

It's been three years since I was a reference librarian and now I need to come up with a core list of reference tools that I should teach.

I feel pretty good about the Internet core lists that I have (see www.kovacs. com under "Training Support" to see some of the work I've done). But, I need to ask for advice on the print, CD-ROM, Tape, and online database tools.

Please reply to me at diane@kovacs.com. I will summarize for the list.

1. What are the top five print reference books that you can't work without?

2. What are the top three CD-ROM, Tape, or online databases that you can't work without?

With Questions two to six, any type of tool that is your most used for this type of question will be helpful.

3. What are your two most used reference tools for business questions?

4. What are your two most used reference tools for medical questions?

5. What are your two most used reference tools for jobs and employment questions?

6. What are your two most used reference tools for law questions?

I appreciate any help you can give me as I'm writing a book chapter about creating Internet e-libraries using the same strategies for selection development that we use for other library collections and I'm writing a proposal to do Internet, print, and other electronic reference training for public librarians in my state.

Figure 2.2.   May 25, 1999 Question Posted to Libref-L and Publib

Revisiting Core Reference Tools?
Diane K. Kovacs (diane@kovacs.com)
Tue, 25 May 1999 22:52:38 -0700 (PDT)

Dear Publib Folks,

Last spring I was writing a grant project for which I needed to have my memory refreshed about core reference tools. This spring our grant project was funded so we're teaching a pilot course "Introduction to Learning Entre-preneurship" to train library paraprofessionals in basic traditional and Inter-net reference sources, computer literacy, and communications skills. I'm happy to share the syllabus with anyone who asks me. I don't want to put it up on the Web until we've finalized it. This course will be the orientation course for a complete paraprofessional associates degree program that we're also developing. The course was approved for three hours credit at Belmont Technical College in Ohio to be taught in July 1999. So I'd appreciate your advice again. Here is the message I sent last spring. I appreciate any and all suggestions:

It's been three years since I was a reference librarian and now I need to come up with a core list of reference tools that I should teach. I feel pretty good about the Internet core lists that I have (see www.kovacs.com to see some of the work I've done). But, I need to ask for advice on the print, CD-ROM, Tape, and online database tools.

Please reply to me at diane@kovacs.com. I will summarize for the list.

1. What are the top five print reference books that you can't work without?
2. What are the top three CD-ROM, Tape, or online databases that you can't work without?

With Questions two to six, any type of tool that is your most used for this type of question will be helpful.

3. What are your two most used reference tools for business questions?
4. What are your two most used reference tools for medical questions?
5. What are your two most used reference tools for jobs and employment questions?
6. What are your two most used reference tools for law questions?

Figure 2.3   June 15, 1999 Report on Core Reference Tools Posted to Libref-L and Publib

Date: Tue, 15 Jun 1999 13:10:35 -0400
Subject: Survey Results: Core Reference Tools

===== Original Message From "Diane K. Kovacs" <diane@kovacs.com> =====

Thank you all very much to everyone who responded. Here are the core reference tools survey results from my previous question to this list (sorry for cross-posting inconveniences). They are in approximately order of their mention with some notes from me and comments from respondents. Please feel free to send me your core reference tools. I can always add to these. Thank you all again!

1. What are the top five print reference books that you can't work without?

The top seven:
World Almanac (comment: "hardcover, because I don't have to remove my
    glasses to read tables, etc.")
World Book Encyclopedia
Encyclopedia of Associations
Random House 2nd ed. Unabridged Dictionary
Encyclopedia Britannica
Statistical Abstracts
Local/Regional and major city phone books

The also rans:
National Five-Digit Zip Code and Post Office Directory
NADA automobile price guides, *Kelley Blue Books, Edmunds Used Car Price
    Guide*
Haines Criss-Cross Directory
Thomas Register
American Heritage English Dictionary
Americana Encyclopedia
CIA World Factbook
Consumer's Reports (both the magazines and the annual buying guides)
Contemporary Black Biography. (We have a large African American popula-
    tion, and this series is great for Black History Month.)
Directory of Corporate Affiliations
Endangered Wildlife of the World (Marshall Cavendish)
Infotrac Magazine ASAP (CD-ROM)

International Wildlife Encyclopedia (Marshall Cavendish)
McGraw-Hill Ency. of World Biography (comment: "though may need updating!")
McGraw-Hill Encyclopedia of Science & Technology
Merck Manual
New York Times Almanac
Physicians Desk Reference *note votes in Medical questions also.
The Information Please series—great starting points for many assignments.
Specific State codes, regulations, and case reporters
DSM-IV
(comment: "It is my firm belief that >90% of reference questions can be answered using only these two sources." speaking of the *Random House Unabridged* and the *World Almanac*).

2. What are the top three CD-ROM, Tape, or online databases that you can't work without?

Infotrac Magazine and *Newspaper Indexes*
PhoneDisc, Powerfinder Phone Discs (or similar product)
American Business Disk
Electric Library
Infotrac Health Reference Center
Amazon.com
Books In Print
EBSCOhost online periodical database
Full text magazine database—UMI or Ebsco. (The more titles in full-text the better.)
Grangers Poetry
IAC magazine indexes (Searchbank—General Reference Center & Health Reference Center)
Local Newspaper (online or CD-ROM) (comments: "we have *Dallas Morning News* CD-ROM or online periodical index such as Infotrak General Reference, Active Dayton (index to the local newspaper)")
Newsbank Comprehensive
MEDLINE
SIRS Researcher
B&T Link database from Baker & Taylor (comment: "similar to BIP on disc, only better.")

Table 2.3 *Continued on Following Page*

Figure 2.3. *Continued*

3. What are your two most used reference tools for business questions?

Southern California Business Directory—provides addresses, contact information, and some sales data for many local businesses. Main directory is by SIC (or whatever the new classification is called)/subject, with geographic, zip code, and alphabetical listings.
ValueLine Investment Survey
Duns Million Dollar Directory
American Business Disk
Dun and Bradstreets Business Directories
Hoover's directories
Standard & Poors Register
Thomas Register of American Manufacturers
Moody's Industrial Manual
Business InfoTrac Online
Directory of Corporate Affiliations
Illinois Services Directory
Infotrac Company Profiles
Morningstar Mutual Fund Survey
Poor's Company Directory
Wisconsin Business Services Directory (published by State Chamber of Commerce)
Wisconsin Manufacturers Directory Plus
California Manufacturers and Service Industry Directories for product complaint—Gale's Brands and their companies

4. What are your two most used reference tools for medical questions?

Merck Manual
PDR
Health Reference InfoTrac
Encyclopedia of Diseases (Springhouse?)
Consumer Reports Complete Drug Reference
Harrison's Principles of Internal Medicine
Pharmacopeia
Stedman's Medical Dictionary

5. What are your two most used reference tools for jobs and employment questions?

The number one source by a lot:
Occupational Outlook Handbook (comment: "Occupational Outlook Handbook is THE most frequently used source, nothing else really comes close.")

Others:
Assortment of resume books kept at reference desk
Internet
Local newspaper help wanted ads
Career Information Center (13v., Macmillan Pub.)
Help Wanted USA (job ads from multiple Sunday papers on microfiche)
Infotrac Company Profiles
Directory of Executive Recruiters
Moody's Manuals (comment: "that huge news collection")
Career Information Center (Ferguson) or Encyclopedia of
    Careers and Vocational Guidance (Macmillan)
Ferguson's Encyclopedia of Careers and Vocational Guidance
American Almanac of Jobs and Salaries
Ohio Industrial Directory

6. What are your two most used reference tools for law questions?

The number one source by a lot:
Specific state codes, regulations, and case reporters.

Others:
West's Encyclopedia of American Law
Nolo Press books on divorce, bankruptcy, copyright, trademark, and patents
Black's Law Dictionary
GPO Access - through internet
Thomas online - through internet
WESTLAW CD-ROM (Massachusetts Laws, Regs, Cases)
Martindale-Hubbel
Tenant/Landlord Law (various sources - mostly local)
Legal Forms publications
BOCA codes (Building Officials and Code Administrators) for regulations on
    various building projects
Divorce in Ohio

Other areas added:
"Two areas I didn't have room for are Native Americans (Encyclopedia of
Native American Tribes by Waldman) and information about what happened
in different eras (Time-Life series of the Gale Decades series)"

These core reference tools fall into some clear categories. The core reference tool types are:

1. Directories—such as the National Five-Digit Zip Code and Post Office Directory, phone books and PhoneDisc, Powerfinder Phone Discs, or similar product.
2. Dictionaries—such as Random House 2nd ed. Unabridged Dictionary or American Heritage English Dictionary.
3. Abstracts, Indexes, and Table of Contents Services—such as Statistical Abstracts, Infotrac Magazine, and Newspaper Indexes.
4. Encyclopedias and Almanacs—such as World Almanac, World Book Encyclopedia, Encyclopedia of Associations, Encyclopedia Britannica, and the subject encyclopedias.
5. Serials and Full-text databases—such as Electric Library, Physicans Desk Reference, Consumer's Reports, and SIRS Researcher.
6. Bibliographies and Bibliographic Databases—such as Amazon.com, Books In Print+, and EBSCOhost online periodical database.
7. News (Current Awareness) sources—such as Local Newspaper (online or CD-ROM)
8. Key Primary Documents—such as Annual Reports, Law Codes, Statistical Sources, etc.).

Using these core ready-reference tools as an "ideal" and the strategies and tools discussed in the section "Identifying and Collecting Internet Resources" in Chapter One of this book, the following core ready-reference e-library collection was created. Most of these sites were found in one or more of the case study e-libraries under their "Ready-Reference" or "Reference" collection headings. LII, MEL, and the OPLIN Websites were most useful.

E-library Builder Stories

Librarians' Index to the Internet (LII)

California State Library
Sacramento, California, USA
www.lii.org/
Carole Leita
leita@lii.org

The Librarians' Index to the Internet (LII) is an excellent collection development tool for librarians building their own e-library. Currently, it includes more than 5,000 Internet sites selected and evaluated by librarians. The criteria for selection and evaluation are described in the document at www.lii.org/InternetIndex/pubcritera.html.

LII began as Carole Leita's Gopher bookmark list back in 1990; later it migrated to her Netscape browser bookmark file. In 1993 she published the Index on the Berkeley Public Library's Web server:

> During this later period I had begun teaching Internet skills to public library staff in California who were part of the state library/LSCA-funded InFoPeople Project. I got to know another instructor (Roy Tennant) who thought the Index would be a great resource to put on the SunSITE server he manages at University of California Berkeley. We began working on it in late 1996 and went up in January 1997 at its present location.

The Berkeley Public Library administration thought it was great, but was unable to support it by giving either staff time or funding. All of the development work was done by Leita on her own time at her own expense. The project is published at www.lii.org and is hosted on the SunSITE server at the University of California–Berkeley.

Leita didn't begin with a written collection plan but later wrote a grant application which clearly explicated the project:

> The first formal written plan for the LII was an LSTA grant proposal submitted to the California State Library for the 1997/98 federal fiscal year. The State Library recognized the value of the LII as a statewide resource and funded the project. Essentially, during that first year of grant funding we proposed the development of a team of volunteer indexers under my direction as well as a variety of technical enhancements. A second grant proposal was submitted, and funded, for the 1998/99 fiscal year. During this year, the emphasis is on: maintaining the core of volunteer indexers at approximately 80; using a paid intern to fill collection gaps, create cross-referencing and various levels of subject pages, and do some editing; enhancing search capabilities.

LII is made searchable by the basic search engine SWISH-E. This required some programming. According to Leita, "Roy Tennant and his team (mostly him) wrote several Perl scripts that process the data."

The first SunSITE server was a SPARCenter 2000E; it is currently running on a Sun Enterprise 3500 running SunOS 2.6 donated by Sun Microsystems, Inc. The Web server software is Apache 1.3.3. As such, there was no major cost for hardware and software. The 1998/99 LSTA grant provides $10,000 for software; Leita has not decided yet what, if any, software will be purchased.

All the initial start-up time, 1990 to 1996, was Leita's unpaid personal time. The 1997/98 and 1998/99 LSTA grants pay for 30 hours a month of her time in expanding and coordinating the LII project, though Leita estimates this " . . . includes working with Roy on enhancements, training the indexers, editing the indexers' entries, writing the manual, maintaining (updating the entries), working on the subject headings, etc."

Leita also estimates that she spends between 40 and 50 more hours a month on the LII than the 30 she is actually paid for. The 1998/99 LSTA grant will also pay for 20 hours a week of an assistant's time. The assistant is currently working on the subject arrangements and will be taking over a share of the editing and updating.

The funding from the LSTA grants also enables Leita to recruit and train volunteers to work on the LII:

> We have trained volunteers who mostly do the work on their own time, although there are many libraries who do allow a certain amount of work time and all the libraries allowed the volunteers work time off for the required day of training. They received a one-day, hands-on workshop. In addition, there is an online manual available at: http://sunsite.berkeley.edu//InternetIndex/manual/

A complete list of all the volunteers who contribute to the LII is available at http://sunsite.berkeley.edu/InternetIndex/indexers.html. In addition, all of the LII entries are signed with the contributor's initials and their initials are linked to this page.

There are currently 68 volunteer indexers who spend an average of four hours a month on the LII.

Leita says, "As part of the plan for 1998/99, the InFoPeople Project Coordinator (the LII is a part of the InFoPeople Project) will work with State Library staff and others to develop a long-range plan for the continuation of the LII. A preliminary LSTA proposal for the 1999/2000 fiscal year has requested funding for someone from the Stanford Business School to develop a business plan for the LII. We are optimistic about the future."

Pinakes: A Subject Launchpad

Heriot-Watt University
Edinburgh, United Kingdom
www.hw.ac.uk/libwww/irn/pinakes/pinakes.html
Roddy MacLeod
R.A.MacLeod@hw.ac.uk

The name Pinakes comes from ancient Greece: In ancient times, the Library of Alexandria was seen as a universal store of human knowl-

About the LII

Digital Library SunSITE

California State Library

Librarians' Index to the Internet

Search word(s): [ ] [Search]

Options: ● ALL ○ Subjects ○ Titles ○ Descriptions
Browse List of Subjects Used | Search tips | Best Search Tools Form

New This Week - Subscribe!
More new... - **New Last Week**

Arts - Architecture | Museums | Performing | more...
Automobiles - Motorcycles
Business - Investing | Taxes | more...
California - Politics | Bay Area : Berkeley | Oakland | San Francisco | Southern California : Los Angeles
Computers - Software | Viruses | more...
Cultures (World) - Anthropology | Africa | Asia | Europe | LatA | MidE | NorA
Current Events
Disabilities
Education - Distance | K-12 | Colleges | Aid | more...
Families - Homes | Moving
Food - Recipes | Restaurants | more...
Gay, Lesbian, Bisexual
Geography - Maps | more...

Government - Federal | International | more...
Health - Diseases | Nutrition | more...
History - Genealogy |
Ancient | Medieval | Military | U.S.
Images, Graphics, Clip Art
Internet Information - Filtering | Evaluation | Training | WWW | more...
Jobs - Listings | Resumes | more...
Kids - Fun | Health | Homework | Internet Safety | Parents | Teachers
Language - English | Spanish | more...
Law - Censorship | Copyright | Crime | more...
Libraries - Public | *for* Librarians
Literature - Authors | Genres | Prizes | Publishers | more...
Media - News | Magazines | Newspapers | Radio | TV
Men
Music - Jazz | Lyrics | Opera | more...
Organizations

People - Collected Biographies
Philosophy
Politics - Elections
Recreation - Games | Gardening | Movies | Outdoor | Pets | more...
Reference Desk - Calendars | Census | Dictionaries | Holidays | Names | Phone Books | Statistics | Time
Religion - Christianity | Islam | Judaism | Mythology | more...
Science - Animals | Astronomy | Environment | Math | Technology | more...
Searching the Internet - more...
Seniors
Sports - Baseball | Olympics | Tennis | more...
Surfing the Internet
Travel - Accommodations | Places | Transportation | more...
Weather - Tides | more...
Women - History | Politics | Studies

The Librarians' Index to the Internet (LII)

edge. As the Library grew in size, however, it became increasingly difficult to locate relevant material. The poet Callimachus solved the problem by compiling a catalogue called The Pinakes. On a far smaller scale, the Pinakes Web pages hope to provide a similar function for Internet resources, by linking to the major subject gateways.

Pinakes: A Subject Launchpad is intended as a starting point for subject searching for Internet resources. Roddy MacLeod, with the support of the Heriot-Watt University Library administration, developed Pinakes as a small but high quality Internet resource collection tool.

"Pinakes is very small scale, (little more than links, with nice graphics and layout to 25 subject gateways) but it's potentially a great starting point for subject searching, and has proved very popular," MacLeod says.

MacLeod didn't produce a written collecting plan, but his overall idea was "to provide a top-level entry point for subject based enquiries, and to publicise the fact that several excellent subject based gateways exist."

Pinakes consists of two simple Web pages that require minimal maintenance. They are published on the Heriot-Watt University's Web server. There was no direct hardware or software cost and the personnel cost was minimal. MacLeod and Dave Bond maintain the pages as part of their regular duties. They are mainly pointing to specific high-quality subject directories of Internet resources. Future developments will include some updating and expansion.

PINAKEΣ
A Subject Launchpad

Subject List

About

Featured in the *BBC Web Wise* guide to the Internet, and many other online and print publications.

Hosted by *Heriot-Watt University* , Edinburgh, Scotland.

ADAM: art, design, architecture and media

Aerospace Resources on the Internet: aerospace information

AHDS: arts and humanities

Biz/ed: business and economics

BUBL: library and information science

CAIN: conflict studies

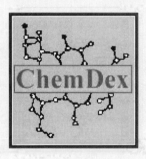

ChemDex: chemistry

EdWeb: educational reform and information technology

Pinakes: A Subject Launchpad

Print and Electronic Publications Cited or Consulted in Chapter Two

Baldwin, C.M. and Mitchell, S., 1996. "Collection Issues and Overview." Untangling the Web. (www.library.ucsb.edu/untangle/baldwin.html).

Fales, S. L., Ed. 1996. *Guide for Training Collection Development Librarians*. Collection Management and Development Guides. No 8. Chicago: American Library Association.

Kaag, C. S. 1998. "Collection Development of Online Serials: Who Needs to Do What, and Why, and When." *Serials Librarian*. 33, nos 1–2: 107–122.

Kovacs, D. and Elkordy, A. "Collection Development in Cyberspace: Building and Electronic Library Collection. *Library Hi-Tech*. (forthcoming)

Mitchell, S. and Mooney, M. 1996. "INFOMINE A Model Web-based Academic Virtual Library." Information Technology and Libraries. (http://infomine.ucr.edu/pubs/italmine.html).

Mogge, D. and Kovacs, D. 1998. *ARL Directory of Electronic Journals, Newsletters Academic Discussion Lists*. Washington, D.C.: Association of Research Libraries. (www.arl.org/scomm/edir/).

Oder, N. 1998. "Cataloging the Net: Can We Do It." *Library Journal*. 123, no 16: 47–51.

Sowards, S. W. 1998. "A Typology for Ready Reference Websites in Libraries."*First Monday*. 1, no 14. (www.firstmonday.dk/issues/).

Walter, W. H., Demas, S. G., Stewart, L., Weintraub, J. 1998. "Collecting Aggregations of Web Resources."*Information Technology and Libraries*. 17, no 3: 157–160.

Websites Cited in Chapter Two (some of these are also listed with annotations in the Webliographies)

MEL – Michigan Electronic Library (http://mel.lib.mi.us)
OPLIN – Ohio Public Information Network (www.oplin.lib.oh.us)

Webliographies Included with Chapter Two

ACCRI-L
Discussion of Internet resources for anesthesiology and critical care.
Archives: Contact the moderator for details
Subscribe: Send e-mail to listserve@uabdpo.dpo.uab.edu with the command:
    Subscribe accri-l yourname
Contact: AJ Wright meds 002@uadbpo.dpo.uab.edu

ACQNET
Discussion for acquisitions and collection development librarians.
Archives: www.library.vanderbilt.edu/law/acqs/acqs.html
Subscribe: Send e-mail to listserv@listserve.appstate.edu with the command:
    Subscribe acqnet yourname
Contact: EleanorCook cookei@appstate.edu

ASIA-WWW-MONITOR
Discusses websites for social science studies in and about Asia.
Archives: http://coombs.anu.edu.au/asia-www-monitor.html
Subscribe: Send e-mail to majordomo@coombs.anu.edu.au with the command:
    subscribe asia-www-monitor youremailaddress
Contact: Dr T.Matthew Ciolek tmciolek@coombs.anu.edu.au

BIOSCI
Group of bio-science discussion lists and newsgroups.
Subscribe: www.bio.net/
Contact: biosci-help@net.bio.net

Buslib-L
Moderated electronic forum that addresses all issues relating to: the collection, storage and dissemination of business information within a library setting—regardless of format.
Archives and Subscribe: www.willamette.edu/~gklein/buslib.htm
Contact: Gary Klein

Cancerwire
(www.rwneill.com/publishing/)
Cancerwire is an e-newsletter which publishes general cancer news, clinical trials, support groups, Internet resource reviews, and other information for cancer patients, caregivers, and medical professionals.

Subscribe: www.rwneill.com/publishing/
Contact: www.rwneill.com/publishing/

COLLDV-L
Moderated: discussion for library collection development officers, bibliographers, and selectors plus others involved with library collection development, including interested publishers and vendors.
Subscribe: Send e-mail to listserv@vm.usc.edu with the command: subscribe
     colldv-l yourname
Contact: Lynn Sipe lsipe@calvin.usc.edu

CONSDIST
Discussion of collection and preservation of library, archives, and museum materials.
Archives: http://palimpsest.stanford.edu/byform/mailing-lists/cdl
Subscribe: Send e-mail to consdist-request@lindy.stanford.edu
Contact: Walter Henry consdist-request@lindy.stanford.edn

COOMBSWeb Social Sciences
http://coombs.anu.edu.au/CoombsHome.html

ECOLL
Subscribe: send e-mail to listproc@unllib.unl.edu with the command: Subscribe ecoll

Edresource
Discussion of the education resources available that benefit Internet educators.
Subscribe and Archives: www.egroups.com/list/edresource
Contact: Arun Tripathi, tripath-@amadeus.statistik.uni-dortmund.de

ELDNET
Discussion of the Engineering Libraries Division of the American Society of Engineering Education.
Subscribe: Send e-mail to listserv@ukans.edu with the command: subscribe
     eldnet yourname
Contact: desart@falcon.cc.ukans.edu

Feminist Collections
(www.library.wisc.edu/libraries/WomensStudies/fcmain.htm)
Publishes reviews of Internet resources related to women's studies in the arts, humanities, social sciences and sciences

The Finger Searcher Science Seeker Newsletter
(www.connect.ab.ca/~xdr/fsearch/fsindex.html)
Publishes nothing but reviews of science resources on the Internet. Again the Internet Scout Project (http://scout.cs.wisc.edu/) comes through for physical sciences researchers and educators by publishing The Scout Report for Science and Engineering. This bi-weekly e-newsletter publishes reviews of Internet resources of interest to researchers and educators in the physical and life sciences fields.

HMATRIX-L
Focuses entirely on health and medical resources on the Internet.
Archives: Contact the moderator for details.
Subscribe: Send e-mail to listserv@knmchttp.mc.ukans.edn with the command:
    Subscribe hmatrix-l yourname
Contact: Lee Hancock le07144@ukanvm.cc.ukans.edu

InSITE
(www.lawschool.cornell.edu/lawlibrary/insite.html)
An e-serial which reviews and annotates Internet legal information Websites. It is published by the Cornell Law Library.

Law-Lib
Discussion for law librarians.
Archives: www.ljx.com/public/mailinglists/uclaw-lib/index.html
Subscribe: Send e-mail to listproc@ucdavis.edu with the command: subscribe
    law-lib your name
Contact: Judy Janes jcjanes@ucdavis.edu

The Law Library Resource Exchange
(www.llrx.com)
An outstanding current awareness 'webzine' which not only publishes legal Website reviews but also publishes articles discussing all aspects of legal information on the Internet.

Lawlibref-l
Discussion for law reference librarians working in all types of libraries.
Archives: www.ljx.com/public/mailinglists/wwwlawlibref-l/index.html
Subscribe: Send e-mail to listproc@lawlib.wujacc.edu with the command:
    subscribe lawlibref-l your name
Contact: Lissa Lord zzlord@acc.wuacc.edu

LAWSRC-L
Internet Law Resources List
Subscribe: Send e-mail to listproc@law.cornell.edu with the command: subscribe lawsrc-l your name

Library and Information Sciences Gopher Server Jewels

Libref-L
Discussion of library reference concepts, issues, and service.
Archives: http://listserv.kent.edu/archives/libref-l.html
Subscribe: Send e-mail to listserv@listserv.kent.edu with the command: subscribe Libref-L your name
Contact: Diane K. Kovacs diane@kovacs.com

LM_NET
Subscribe: Send e-mail to listserv@listserv.syr.edu with the command: subscribe lm_net Yourname
Contact: Mike Eisenberg mike@ericir.syr.edu or Peter Milbury pmilbury@cusd.chico.k12.ca.us

MATHQA
Discussion list which includes reviews of mathematical Websites.
Archives: Contact the moderator for details.
Subscribe: Send e-mail to majordomo@lists.oulu.fi with the message: Subscribe mathqa your e-mail address
Contact: Nick Halloway snow@rain.org

MEDLIB-L
Discussion list for medical librarians which includes discussion of Internet resources for medical e-library collection.
Archives: Contact the moderator for details.
Subscribe: Send e-mail to listserv@listserv.acsu.buffalo.edu with the message: Subscribe medlib-1 yourname
Contact: Jan Mixter jmixter@luc.edu

Net-Happenings
Announcements of new Internet resources and excerpts from various discussions of Internet-related events.
Archives: http://scout.cs.wisc.edu/scout/caservices/new-list/index.html
Subscribe: Send e-mail to listserv@hypatia.cs.wisc.edu with the command: subscribe net-happenings your name

or
fill out the form at http://scout18.cs.wisc.edu/cgi-bin/lwgate/listsavail.html
or
use a Usenet Newsreader to access comp.internet.net-happenings
Contact: Gleason Sackman gleason@rrnet.com

NetInLib-Announce
Current awareness service whose purpose is to alert librarians and other information professionals to new, innovative, or useful Internet resources. Members can announce resources they feel are worth sharing.
Subscribe: www.targetinform.com/netinlib/
Contact: Mark Jordan mjordan@mail.bc.rogers.wave.ca

NewJour
NEWNIR-L
New network resource announcements.
Distribution list for the announcement of new electronic journals and newsletters.
Archives: http://gort.ucsd.edu/newjour/
Subscribe: submit the form at http://gort.ucsd.edu/newjour/subscribe.html
Contact: owner-newjour@ccat.sas.upenn.edu

PHOAKS
The PHOAKS project.
www.phoaks.com

PSYCHIATRY-RESOURCES
Discussion list for review and recommendation of Psychiatry information on and off the Internet.
Archives: Contact the moderator for details.
Subscribe: Send e-mail to listserv@maelstrom.stjohns.edu with the message:
     Subscribe psychiatry-resources yourname
Contact: Myron Pulier mpulier@interport.net

PUBLIB
Discussion of issues relating to public librarianship. "Particularly appropriate issues for discussion on PUBLIB include, but are not limited to: Collection development, acquisitions, management, and weeding, including traditional and new media reference services . . . "
Archives: http://sunsite.berkeley.edu/PubLib/archive.html
Subscribe: Send the message "subscribe PUBLIB YourFirstName YourLastName" to listserv@sunsite.berkeley.edu

Contact: Sara Weissman weissman@main.morris.org or
Karen Schneider kgs@bluehighways.com

PUBLIB-NET
A sublist of PUBLIB where discussion is devoted strictly to the Internet in
public libraries.
Archives: http://sunsite.berkeley.edu/PubLib/archive.html
Subscribe: send the message "subscribe PUBLIB-NET YourFirstName
    YourLastName" to listserv@sunsite.berkeley.edu
Contact: Sara Weissman weissman@main.morris.org or
Karen Schneider kgs@bluehighways.com

The Scout Report
(http://scout.cs.wisc.edu/index.html)
Weekly e-newsletter distribution which publishes reviews of Internet resources
of interest to researchers and educators. Different versions include SCOUT-
REPORT-HTML, The Scout Report HTML version. The subject-specific ver-
sions are described in Chapters 3, 4, and 5.
Subscribe: Fill out the form at http://scout18.cs.wisc.edu/cgi-bin/lwgate/
    listsavail.html
Archives: http://scout.cs.wisc.edu/report/sr/archive/index.html
Contact: scout-report-request@cs.wisc.edu

SLA-Dite
Discussion for the Information Technology Division of the Special Libraries
Association
Subscribe: Send e-mail to listserv@listserv.sla.org with the command: subscribe
    sla-dite yourname
Contact: Hope N. Tillman hope@tiac.net

SOHO-SPIDER
Reviews Websites of interest to small business.
Subscribe: Send e-mail to majordomo@sohoweb.net with the command: sub-
    scribe soho-spider youremailaddress
Contact: Scott Temaat spider@sohoweb.net

The Spire Project Australia
(http://cn.net.au)
The Spire Project is uniquely not a library-based project. It is a subject guide
to information research, released as FAQ, shareware, Website, and for publishing on other Websites. The information is organized as a collection of
research strategy articles covering topics like patent research and country pro-

files. The work is prepared by David Novak, a professional researcher and manager of Community Networking (Australia), with his wife Fiona.
Contact: David Novak david@cn.net.au

SRBUSECON, The Scout Report for Business and Economics
Bi-weekly e-newsletter distribution which publishes reviews of Internet resources of interest to researchers and educators in the business and economics fields.
Subscribe: Fill out the form at http://scout18.cs.wisc.edu/cgi-bin/lwgate/
    listsavail.html
Archives: http://scout.cs.wisc.edu/report/sr/archive/index.html
Contact: SRBusEcon-request@cs.wisc.edu

SRSCIENG, The Scout Report for Science and Engineering
Bi-weekly e-newsletter distribution which publishes reviews of Internet resources of interest to researchers and educators in the physical and life sciences fields.
Subscribe: Fill out the form at http://scout18.cs.wisc.edu/cgi-bin/lwgate/
    listsavail.html
Archives: http://scout.cs.wisc.edu/report/sr/archive/index.html
Contact: SRSciEng-request@cs.wisc.edu

SRSOCSCI, The Scout Report for Social Sciences
Bi-weekly e-newsletter distribution which publishes reviews of Internet resources of interest to researchers and educators in the social sciences.
Subscribe: Fill out the form at http://scout18.cs.wisc.edu/cgi-bin/lwgate/
    listsavail.html
Archives: http://scout.cs.wisc.edu/report/sr/archive/index.html
Contact: SRSocSci-request@cs.wisc.edu

STS-L
Discussion of science and technology librarianship.
Subscribe: Send e-mail to listserv@utkvm1.utk.edu with the command:
    subscribe sts-l yourname
Contact: Marty Courtois mpc@gwu.edu

Web4Lib
Discussion of the practical use and philosophical issues of the World Wide Web in library contexts.
Archives: http://sunsite.berkeley.edu/Web4Lib/archive.html
Subscribe: send e-mail to listproc@sunsite.berkeley.edu with the message: subscribe web4lib yourfirstname yourlastname

Contact: Roy Tennant rtennant@library.berkeley.edu or
Thomas Dowling tdowling@ohiolink.edu.

Collection Development Related Discussion Groups, E-serials and Guides, Evaluation Guides, and Workshops

Answering Reference Questions Using the Internet
www.bcpl.gov.bc.ca/workshop/table.htm
Contact: Joel Minion, jminion@hq.marh.gov.bc.ca
Question & Answer format at top, then lots of info and one-line remarks about different Internet reference sites for librarians.

Bibliography on Evaluating Internet Resources
http://refserver.lib.vt.edu/libinst/critTHINK.HTM
Contact: Nicole Auer, auern@vt.edu
This bibliography addresses "the problems and issues related to teaching and using critical thinking skills to evaluate Internet resources." Internet and Print resources, and useful Listservs.

Bobby
www.cast.org/bobby
Bobby is a tool that allows you to submit any URL and evaluates its accessibility to everyone regardless of physical handicaps. It is also an HTML validation tool.

Evaluating Web Resources
www.science.widener.edu
Contact: Jan Alexander, Janet.E.Alexander@widener.edu or
Marsha Ann Tate, Marsha.A.Tate@widener.edu
Provides materials to assist in teaching how to evaluate the informational content of Web resources.

Guide to Web Style
www.wswest2.sun.com/styleguide/
Contact: Rick Levine, rick.levine@Sun.COM
Examines the issues of etiquette, content, and quality of Websites. Describes the effectiveness of links and image maps. Lists some overused buzzwords.

Privacy Test Sites
www.mall-net.com/cgibin/whoami.cgi?src=webcons
www.privacy.net
These two sites are online tools that check all the privacy access points on the system from which you connect to the Internet.

Teaching Students to Think Critically about Internet Resources
http://weber.u.washington.edu/~libr560/NETEVAL/
Contact: Andrea Bartelstein, andi@u.washington.edu or Anne Zald, zald@u.washington.edu
A Workshop for faculty and TAs.

The Complete Internet Researcher
www.law.ab.umd.edu/marshall/workshop/index.html
Contact: Elliot Chabot, elliot.chabot@mail.house.gov or Sheri H. Lewis, lewis_sh@Mercer.EDU
Advanced strategies and techniques for ascertaining information quality and developing research strategies and other Internet skills.

Publishers Wanted, No Experience Necessary: Information Quality on the Web
www.llrx.com/columns/quality.htm
Contact: Genie Tyburski, tyburski@hslc.org
Column from the Law Library Resource Exchange. Methods for identifying information quality on the Web.

Criteria for Evaluating Information Resources
www.usc.edu/isd/locations/science/sci/pubs/criteval.html
Contact: Julie Kwan, nhanel@usc.edu
Questions to ask in order to assess sources and analyze the results; no links.

Evaluation Center
www.edsoasis.org/Guidelines.html
Contact: Terrie Gray, Director; tgray@pepperdine.edu
An online instructional resource guidelines to determine effective education sites.

Evaluating World Wide Web Information
http://thorplus.lib.purdue.edu/research/classes/gs175/
3gs175/evaluation.html
Contact: Ann Scholz, scholz@sage.cc.purdue.edu
Guide for evaluating the World Wide Websites and other Internet information.

Evaluation of Information Sources
www.vuw.ac.nz/~agsmith/evaln/evaln.htm
Contact: Alastair Smith, Alastair.Smith@vuw.ac.nz
Criteria for evaluating information resources, particularly those on the Internet.

Evaluating Internet Resources
http://web.wn.net/~usr/ricter/web/valid.html
Contact: Richard Terass, ricter@wn.net
Part of the Medical Radiography Website. This has annotated links to Internet resources of evaluation—many listed on this chart.

Evaluating and Presentations on the Net
www.tiac.net/users/hope/Presentations/presentations.html
Contact: Hope N. Tillman, hope@tiac.netne
Links to different presentations relating to evaluating quality and evaluators of the Internet as well as other discussion topics of resources, searches, graphics, tricks, and tips of the Internet.

Evaluating Websites
http://trochim.human.cornell.edu/webeval/webeval.htm
Contact: William Trochim, wmt1@cornell.edu
Variety of evaluation questions and methods.

Finding Quality Sources on the WWW
www.lboro.ac.uk/info/training/finding/finding_quality.html#Webpages
Contact: Alison McNab, A.S.McNab@iboro.ac.uk
Collection of sources (links) relating evaluations, reviews, and quality issues of Web pages and Websites.

Information Quality WWW Virtual Library
www.ciolek.com/WWWVL-InfoQuality.html
Contact: Dr. T. Matthew Ciolek, tmciolek@ciolek.com or Irena M. Goltz, irena.goltz@brs.gov.au
This set of pages keeps track of online resources relevant for evaluation, development, and administration of high quality factual/scholarly networked information systems.

Internet Detective
http://sosig.ac.uk/desire/internet-detective.html
Contact: Emma Worsfold, emma.worsfold@bristol.ac.uk
Interactive tutorial on evaluating the quality of Internet resources.

Internet Technology Training
http://thorplus.lib.purdue.edu/~techman/
Contact: D. Scott Brandt, techman@purdue.edu
Source for technology-training related research and applications in an information retrieving environment.

Internet Validation Project
www.stemnet.nf.ca/Curriculum
Contact: edu6662@calvin.stemnet.nf.ca
This project helps students and teachers who want to use the Internet as a source of information for research papers by providing this set of guidelines.

Manal El-Tigi
http://web.syr.edu/~maeltigi/Research/RIGHT.HTM
Contact: maeltigi@mailbox.syr.edu
A collection of research papers and surveys relating to Website evaluation.

Publishing on the Web
http://www0.delphi.com/pubweb/
Contact: Walt Howe, walthowe@delphi.com
All the information needed to create quality Web pages.

Ten C's for Evaluating Internet Resources
www.uwec.edu/admin/library/10cs.html
Contact: Betsy Richmond, richmoeb@uwec.edu
Ten easy criteria guide evaluations.

Testing the Surf: Criteria for Evaluating Internet Information Resources
http://info.lib.uh.edu/pr/v8/n3/smit8n3.html
Contact: Alastair Smith, Alastair.Smith@vuw.ac.nz
Article from The Public-Access Computer Systems Review (PACS Review) which compares evaluation criteria for print and CD-ROM resources with the criteria needed to evaluate Internet resources; bibliography and links.

Multi-subject Reviewed or Annotated Web Resource Directories and Electronic Library Collections

About.com
www.about.com
Contact: reachus@about-inc.com
Six hundred guides mining the net on thousands of topics—academic and popular.

Alphasearch
www.calvin.edu/library/as
Contact: remelt@calvin.edu

Search by word or phrase for reviewed gateway sites; browse them by resource type, discipline, or alphabetical listing.

The ARL Directory of Electronic Journals, Newsletters, and Academic Discussion Lists
www.arl.org/scomm/edir/

The Argus Clearinghouse
www.clearinghouse.net
Contact: clearinghouse@argus-inc.com
Sites are annotated, reviewed, and rated by subject experts (librarians). Search or browse the hierarchically arranged directory.

Barnes Learning Resource Center
www.galter.nwu.edu/libinfo/lrc
Contact: galter-lrc@nwu.edu.
The LRC houses the library's non-print collection, including anatomical models, computers, software (including word processing and e-mail), computer-aided instruction (CAI) resources, videocassettes, audiocassettes, interactive laser videodiscs, both audio and multimedia CD-ROMs, and 35mm slides.

Bartlesville Public Library
www.bartlesville.lib.ok.us/
Contact: webmast@bartlesville.lib.ok.us
Full Service online library

Beaucoup
www.beaucoup.com
Contact: Teri Madden, webmaster@beaucoup.com
Over 2,500 search sites, including topics of parallel/Meta, Reviewed/What's New, Music, Science, Health, Employment, etc.; coming soon, searching the search engines.

Beyond Bookmarks: Schemes for Organizing the Web
www.public.iastate.edu/~CYBERSTACKS/CTW.htm
Contact: Gerry Mckiernan, GMCKIERN@gwgate.lib.iastate.edu

Beyond the Black Stump
http://home.mira.net/~lions/anew.htm
Contact: Adam Todd, commercial@au.net
Lists the latest/newest Websites in reverse chronological order. Also search WWW by category.

BUBL/5:15
http://bubl.ac.uk/link/
Contact: Alan Dawson, a.dawson@strath.ac.uk or bubl@bubl.ac.uk
Relevant, librarian-evaluated resources on all academic subject areas.

California Digital Library
www.cdlib.org/
Contact: John Ober, John.Ober@ucop.edu
An integrated Web gateway to digital collections, services, and tools.

Choice - Current Reviews for Academic Libraries
www.ala.org/acrl/choice
www.ala.org/acrl/choice/98sup.html
Contact: Irving E. Rockwood, IRockwood@ala-choice.org
"Timely," "concise," "authoritative," and "easy-to-use" reviews by experts
of books and electronic media.

CyberStacks
www.public.iastate.edu/~CYBERSTACKS
Contact: gerrymck@iastate.edu
Centralized, integrated, and unified collection of significant World Wide Web
(WWW) and other Internet resources categorized using the Library of Congress classification scheme. This service emphasizes the fields of science and
technology, but other topics are now available, such as geography, medicine,
social science, and law.

The Internet Tourbus
www.tourbus.com
Contact: Patrick Douglas Crispen, crispen@netsquirrel.com or Bob Rankin,
    bobrankin@ulster.net
TOURBUS is a virtual tour of the best of the Internet, delivered by e-mail to
over 80,000 people in 120 countries.

Learning @ Web.Sites
www.ecnet.net/users/gdlevin/home.html
Contact: d-levin@govst.edu.
Searchable guide intended primarily for senior high school educators who
would like to enhance their curriculum and instruction using the Internet.

Detroit Public Library
www.detroit.lib.mi.us/
Contact: mktg@detroit.lib.mi.us

Artwork was developed from actual bits of the library architecture, which is a way to connect the physical location to their comprehensive virtual services.

Digital Librarian
www.servtech.com/~mvail/home.html
Contact: Margaret Vail Anderson, mvail@servtech.com
A librarian's choice for best of the Web.

Directory of Networked Resources
www.niss.ac.uk/subject2/
Contact: niss@niss.ac.uk
Search alphabetically, by subject or by "UDC"(library shelf classifications). Many gateways available at this site.

Directory of Scholarly and Professional Electronic Conferences
www.arl.org/scomm/edir//scomm/edir/

Electronic Libraries Programme
www.ukoln.ac.uk/services/elib/
Contact: elib@ukoln.ac.uk
Information on workshops, studies, and conferences.

eGroups
www.egroups.com/
Join a discussion group regarding specific areas of interest (education, business, humanities, etc.) or start one of your own.

Encyclopedia Britannica Internet Guide
www.britannica.com
Contact: editor@britannica.comtechnical or webmaster@britannica.com
Classifies, rates, and reviews thousands of Websites then clearly and concisely describes, rates according to consistent standards, and indexes for easy retrieval.

Gelman Library
www.gwu.edu/~gelman/subjects/subjects.htm
Contact: Martin Courtois, courtois@gwu.edu
Internet resources divided into five categories then subdivided to more specific topics. Also links to a virtual reference desk.

Infomine: Scholarly Internet Resource Collections
http://lib-www.ucr.edu/
Contact: Steve Mitchell, Co-coordinator; smitch@citrus.ucr.edu or Margaret Mooney, Co-coordinator; mmooney@citrus.ucr.edu

INFOMINE contains over 14,000 links. Substantive databases, electronic journals, guides to the Internet for most disciplines, textbooks, and conference proceedings are among the many types of resources.

Internet Library for Librarians
www.itcompany.com/inforetriever/
Contact: Vianne Tang Sha, ShaW@missouri.edu
A comprehensive Web database designed to provide a one-stop shopping center for librarians to locate Internet resources related to their profession. (Reference, Collection Development, Archives, Administration, Automation, etc.)

Internet Public Library
www.ipl.org/
Contact: ipl@ipl.org
Huge site with many easy-to-use features, including: youth, teen, and just-for-librarians sections, virtual exhibits, and reference collection (with Ask-A-Question feature).

The Internet Sleuth
www.isleuth.com/
Contact: feedback@isleuth.com
Search over 3,000 annotated databases, categorized subjects (not reviewed).

KnowledgeCite Library
www.knowledgecite.com/
Contact: marcr@knowledgecite.com
Limited to individuals affiliated with one of our subscribing institutions. A reference tool providing multi-disciplinary searching across dozens of research-grade databases in a Web environment.

Librarian's Index to the Internet
http://sunsite.berkeley.edu/InternetIndex
Contact: Carole Leita, cleita@sunsite.berkeley.edu
Evaluated, annotated, and searchable collection of Internet resources (academic and popular) organized by subject.

Librarians' Resource Centre
www.sla.org/chapter/ctor/toolbox/resource/index.html
Contact: Margaret Gross, mgross@cam.org
Selective collection of information, resources, and databases organized by clients' needs—public service, professional, and technical.

The Library of Congress
http://lcweb.loc.gov/library
Contact: lcweb@loc.gov
Services for researchers, publishers, and educators; many collections.

Library Spot
www.libraryspot.com/
Contact: feedback@libraryspot.com
Link to law, medical, musical libraries, as well as online libraries; other features include archives, reading room, and librarians' shelf (tools, humor, career info, and more).

MindSpring Enterprises
http://corpcom.mspring.net/corpcom/cgi-bin/query-formb.cgi
Contact: www.mindspring.net/mail.html
Search for sites from a large category list, both academic and popular subjects.

Morrisville College Library
www.morrisville.edu/pages/library/
Contact: Wilfred Drew, drewwe@morrisville.edu
General, specialized (authorization needed on some), and periodical databases.

MEL - Michigan Electronic Library
http://mel.lib.mi.us
Contact: Sue Davidsen, Director; davidsen@umich.edu
Browse the Internet by subject and use the electronic reference desk at this Website.

National Library of Australia
www.nla.gov.au
Contact: Rod Stroud, rstroud@nla.gov.au
Selective subject lists of evaluated Internet resources that are easy to browse. Also contains subject lists of e-mail discussion groups, online newspapers by country, and reference materials.

National Library of Canada - Electronic Collection
http://collection.nlc-bnc.ca/e-coll-e/index-e.htm
Contact: e.publications.e@nlc-blc-ca
The beginnings of an electronic collection which incorporates
formally published Canadian online books and journals; comprehensive site directory.

Needle in a CyberStack
http://members.home.net/Albee/
Contact: John Albee, albee@revealed.net
Use the "needle navigator" to locate the database(s) needed from a large selection of options.

The New Athenaeum
http://members.spree.com/athenaeum/mguide1.htm
Contact: Robert J. Tiess, rjtiess@warwick.net.
Metaguide to Internet resource guides developed by libraries and library professionals all over the world.

North Carolina State University Library
www.lib.ncsu.edu/disciplines/index.html
Contact: eric_morgan@ncsu.edu
Listing and links to both research and internet resources by subject.

Pinakes: A Subject Launchpad
www.hw.ac.uk/libWWW/irn/pinakes/pinakes.html
Contact: Dave Bond, d.a.bond@hw.ac.uk or Roddy MacLeod, r.a.macleod@
    hw.ac.uk
This Website is a set of "graphic" links (easy to use) to the "major subject gateways."

Lycos - Top Five Percent
http://point.lycos.com/categories/index.html
Contact: webmaster@lycos.com
Top Five Percent is a directory of reviewed sites. Search or browse by broad subject arranged by rankings. Mix of popular and academic resources.

Ramapo Catskills Library System
www.rcls.org/
Contact: Jerry Kuntz, jkuntz@rcls.org
Electronic library consisting of search tools (kids search tools), directories, and multiple subject database listings.

Rettig on Reference
www.gale.com
Reviews of traditional and Internet resources for reference by James Rettig. Monthly publication from Gale Research is available free of charge to all Internet users.

ROADS (Resource Organisation And Discovery in Subject-based Services)
www.ukoln.ac.uk/roads/
Contact: roads-liaison@bris.ac.uk
The software allows you to set up a subject gateway.

The Scout Report
http://scout.cs.wisc.edu/scout/report/
Contact: scout@cs.wisc.edu.
Published every Friday both on the Web and by e-mail, it provides a fast, convenient way to stay informed of valuable resources on the Internet. Our team of professional librarians and subject matter experts select, research, and annotate resource.

Seattle Public Library
www.spl.lib.wa.us/
Contact: Deborah L. Jacobs, city.librarian@spl.org
Full service library with online databases, quick information center, reference, etc.

Services to Librarians
www.library.okstate.edu/dept/dls/prestamo/anne5.htm
Contact: Anne Prestamo, prestam@notes.okstate.edu
Database of information for librarians: resources for net training (many areas), references, periodicals, listservs, and libraries.

State Library of Ohio - World Wide Web Information Network
http://winslo.state.oh.us/
Contact: Georgiana Van Syckle, webmaster@winslo.state.oh.us
Lists state and federal government information, online databases, and Ohio Public Library Online (OPLIN).

Schools and Libraries Division
www.slcfund.org/
Contact: question@slcfund.org
Site for school and library regarding funding information, announcements, and forms.

Scout Select Bookmarks: Subject-based Metasites
wwwscout.cs.wisc.edu/scout/toolkit/bookmarks/
Contact: scout@cs.wisc.edu.
Very selective list (chosen for selectivity, breadth, and depth of coverage scope and authority) of metasites in seven academic fields.

Scout Report Signpost
www.signpost.org/signpost/
Contact:signpost@cs.wisc.edu
Searchable, browseable (sic) database of the Scout Report—critical summaries of internets and mailing lists.

Social Science Information Gateway
http://sosig.ac.uk/welcome.htmlor
http://scout18.cs.wisc.edu/sosig_mirror/
Contact: Nicky Ferguson, Director; nicky.ferguson@bris.ac.uk
SOSIG is an online catalogue of thousands of high quality Internet resources relevant to social science education and research. Every resource has been selected and described by a librarian or subject specialist.

Virtual Visit of the Multimedia Library
http://mediatheque.ircam.fr/infos/vrml/index-e.html
Contacts: http://mediatheque.ircam.fr/messages/mail.html
Need to download special software to view/use the "virtual" library. Can access without this, though. Heavy emphasis on music.

World Wide Web Virtual Library
www.vlib.org/Home.html
Individuals maintain the separate collections of this library at separate locations. Contact person listed at each site. Oldest catalog on the Web. Annotated collection of searchable Internet resources arranged by subject.

Ready-reference Metasites

Eurekalert Reference Desk
www.eurekalert.org/resources/
Collection of scientific dictionaries and glossaries in the physical and biological sciences.

Information Please: Online Dictionary, Internet Encyclopedia, & Almanac Reference
www.infoplease.com

Online Reference Tools
www.earlham.edu/~libr/resource/reftools.htm
Contact: webcreator@earlham.edu
Graphic-free, reference, and general information directory.

Internet Quick Reference
www.indiana.edu/~librcsd/internet/
Alphabetic listing of both reference databases and academic databases; searchable.

Ready Reference Collection
www.ipl.org/ref/RR/
Contact: ipl@ipl.org
Huge annotated collection, chosen to help answer specific questions quickly and efficiently. This directory includes links to other topics than basic reference material.

Ready Reference Using the Internet
www.winsor.edu/library/rref.htm
Contact: Ellen Berne, eberne@tiac.net
Large "dictionary-type" annotated listing of academic (not necessarily reference) topics and their database links.

Reference Shelf
www.lib.upenn.edu/resources/reference.html
Contact: refshelf@pobox.upenn.edu
Most-used reference sources (links) displayed first and annotated; other reference resources (some relating just to the college) are listed at side bar.

The Gateway to Information: Titles of Useful Resources
www.lib.ohio-state.edu/gateway/
Searchable alphabetic and subject directory of reference titles. The title is annotated if it is online or physically in one of their libraries.

Virtual Library
www.albany.edu/library/reference/
Contact: Laura Cohen, libwww@csc.albany.edu
Not only is this a directory of all types of references, but also includes a link to other reference metasites.

Virtual Ready Reference Collection
http://web.lwc.edu/administrative/library/refu.htm
Contact: Calvin Boyer, cboyer@longwood.lwc.edu
Graphic-free, directory of links to sources from acronyms to Zip Codes.

Virtual Reference Collection (M.I.T.)
http://libraries.mit.edu/services/virtualref.html
Contact: refnet-lib@mit.edu
Each reference category is listed with its corresponding sites.

3
Collecting Web-based Business and Jobs and Employment Information Resources

"The Internet is developing new technologies every day. These technologies invariably affect the customer, and usually *empower* the customer. Augmented by these technologies, customers are evolving into new creatures who do not respond to old philosophies, strategies, and tactics. For example, the Internet has developed a *pull* mentality instead of the classical *push* mentality of classical broadcast media. Web pages generally don't show up on a user's browser unless the user clicked on something to get them. In a broadcast medium, like TV, ads and shows come on whether you want them or not. The only choices are on, off, or change the channel. If you recall the TV show *Outer Limits*, *pull* means that the user finally controls the horizontal, the vertical, and the focus. The user is in command and expects to *stay* in command . . . Internet marketers should recall the old salesman's adage: 'Buyers don't want to be *sold* a shoe, they want to feel they've just *purchased* a pair.'

The Internet may have had its birth in the U.S., but it has quickly outgrown the nation-state mentality. . . . Business must deal with the emerging social constructions of the Internet."

Morris, M.E.S. and Massie, P. 1998. *Cybercareers*. Mountain View, CA. Sun Microsystems Press. p 43-44.

Business and Jobs and Employment Internet Resource Collection and Evaluation

Business resources are some of the most ubiquitous on the Internet. In an effort to attract customers to their Websites businesses are sharing an unprecedented level of information. Company Websites often contain product catalogs, technical support information, company financial data, annual and quarterly reports, and other information. Traditional business information sources are building on this trend by publishing their print directories on the Web. Advertisers have always been the main source of revenue for most publishers of business directories and company, industry, and financial news. The Internet opens a whole new source of advertising revenue for them. As a result, many such publishers have been steadily expanding versions of their publications onto the Web.

Government collectors of business information are using the Web to make this information available to the public and also requiring businesses to use the Internet to submit their required "paperwork" to government agencies. For instance, the U.S. Securities and Exchange Commission requires public companies to submit reports such as 10K or 10Q directly to the Edgar database via the Internet. Business and financial news is also being published on the Web. This type of information is especially sensitive to security issues and quality considerations because it frequently involves financial or private information. Business information on the Internet is primarily found in the form of directories of businesses and industries, stock market quotations and analysis, and business and financial news. The good Internet business directories, such as Hoovers Online (www.hoovers.com), contain business listings along with industry, product, competitors, financial status, contact information, and other basic data. Stock and commodities market information is also available online in real-time or delayed time (15–20 minutes). It is possible to actually make stock and commodity trades through the Internet in real-time. Other kinds of business information include currency and exchange rates, consumer information, small business support resources, product information, catalogs, and customer support services. Electronic commerce (e-commerce) sites where clients can purchase products or book travel plans through the Internet are increasing in number.

Jobs and employment resources are some of the most popular on the Internet. The equivalent of classified listings of jobs all over the world is available for searching and sometimes even online application on the Internet. Margaret Riley Dikel has been compiling the Riley Guide: Employment Opportunities and Jobs Resource on the Internet since 1996 (www.dbm.com/jobguide). It is the ultimate metasite for these types of information on the Internet. The Riley Guide contains a comprehensive collection of job listing Websites organized by type or job, by local, state, or international location, and other criteria. In addition, it contains a collection of employment information sites. There are thousands of job listing Websites. There are sites for every kind of job. Many sites allow individuals to post their resumes in public resume databases. This will not be a useful job-seeking tool for most people. According to Richard Bolles, author of *What Color is Your Parachute the Net Guide* (www.jobhuntersbible.com/), in his "The Resume Fairy Godmother Report," very few resumes posted on the Web are actually viewed by employers:

> Want proof? You'll see it when you come to the chart of statistics on resume-posting sites. Some of the results you'll see there: One famous resume site had 59,283 resumes posted on it, but only 1,366

employers looked at any of those 59,283 during the 90 days previous to the survey; another site had 85,000 resumes, but only 850 employers looked at them; another had 40,000 resumes, but only 400 employers looked at them; another had 26,644 resumes, but only 41 employers looked at them, in the 90 days previous. If you don't find these statistics depressing, I certainly do—and would, even if you multiplied the number of employers by 100 in each case.

What's the problem here? Why doesn't your resume get more attention online? Well, for a resume to achieve results online, some employer:

- has got to be desperate to find someone like you; and
- has got to be at the point, in their search for someone like you, that they are reduced to reading resumes (many employers' least favorite way of filling a position; they'll try anything else, first, since they regard the task of reading resumes as just this side of having a root canal); and then this employer
- has got to go online looking for a resume-posting site (and remember, there are at least 10 million U.S. employers—not to mention other countries—who don't even think of the Internet when it's time to hire); but if they do, then this employer
- has got to stumble across the site where you posted your resume—and there are hundreds of such sites on the Internet; and then this employer
- has got to accidentally stumble across your resume on that site; and then this employer
- has got to take the time and trouble to read it; and then this employer
- has got to take the time and trouble to print it out, in all its blah ASCII sameness; and then this employer
- has got to decide, after studying it, that they like it enough to invite you in. (Note that the survey only said "looked at" the resume, it didn't say "chose." Many employers look at resumes without finding any that they are interested in. Ho boy!).

Bolles goes on to discuss the greater likelihood that the resumes of computer and other technical professionals will have greater success posting their resumes on public resume sites. For other professionals, putting a resume online—preferably on your own Website and then referring to your online resume site in print cover letters or attaching the resume to e-mailed cover letters can be a good strategy. For individuals applying for a job in which some Internet or computer skills are required this strategy demonstrates that you have some basic knowledge of both.

The Internet Business Information Resource Collection Plan

What Purpose Will Your Web-based E-library Collection Serve? For Whom Are You Collecting Business Internet Resources?

This question was discussed in general in Chapter One, but there are some questions particular to business information uses.

Will the library encourage clients to engage in e-commerce activities? Will the library primarily provide access to product catalogs and consumer information (price comparison sites, for example). Will storefronts and stock and commodity trading sites be included directly in the e-library?

Public libraries will want to provide resources focused on the needs of local businesses. They may find that either, or both, small businesses or local major companies are their primary business information clients and will want to collect resources to support those businesses. Many libraries may need to gather a collection of archived historical business information such as annual reports, historical stock market data, and other materials used in academic business studies or business research. Academic libraries will be collecting for students engaged in business studies defined by their parent university or college programs. The collection scope for their business e-library will be defined by the programs offered and the supporting information required by those programs. Special librarians will be collecting resources to support the business in which they work. For example, a company in the chemical industry would need resources related to the production and use of chemicals. The business librarian may need access to some of the fee-based services which provide very current, very detailed, reports and statistics; such as "Company Intelligence" through Dialog's Web interface. School libraries may need to look hard to find age appropriate business information depending on the age of the children the library serves and the curriculum which they support.

Geographical coverage is also an important consideration. A library may wish to provide in-depth support for local, state, provincial, district, regional, or international business interests. In fact, any modern library may find, in our global economy, that their local businesses, students, and other business information clients need access to international business information.

What Business Internet and Other Electronic Resources Will You Link to Through Your E-library?

Business Internet reference tools take forms that can be described in terms of traditional reference source types. An annotated "Business Core Internet Ready-Reference Collection" at the end of this section lists essential Internet reference tools chosen from these reference source types.

1. Directories of businesses organized by business type, country, state, city, financial status, marketing factors, etc.
2. Dictionaries of business-related terminology. These are not, however, typical business information tools.
3. Bibliographies of Internet business information resources (see the Webliography of Business Resource Metasites at the end of this chapter).
4. Abstracts, indexes, and table of contents service for business serials are generally not freely available on the Internet. Although, many commercial services provide subscription access through the Internet, including the *Wall Street Journal* and *Business Week*. The UnCover database has been available through the Internet for several years. Many business serial contents are searchable through the UnCover database.
5. Business e-serials and full-text databases such as Edgar.
6. Bibliographies and bibliographic databases—see Webliographies of Business Resource Metasites.
7. Business and financial news.
8. Key primary documents such as annual reports, stock, commodities, and industry reports.

In business research, current awareness sources such as journals and news sources are critical and are included in business reference collections. Key primary documents such as stock and commodity reports, financial and statistical reports, marketing reports, and annual reports are also part of the business reference collection.

How Will You Organize Your Internet Business Information Collection?

This question is discussed in general in Chapter One. There is no significant difference between business information and other subject areas that would make the answer to this question different for a business collection than for other subject collections of Internet resources. This question is always going to be answered differently by each library depending on their answers to the first two questions in the collection planning discussion. Most libraries will probably organize business resources by subject. Some might choose to organize by resource type; business serials, business reference tools, and business monographs, for example.

Identifying and Collecting Internet Business Information Resources

Internet business information resources were some of the first to be collected and organized by librarians. In 1994, I assisted my colleague Leslie Haas—now head of the general reference department at the J. W. Marriott Library, University of Utah—in starting to compile the first "Business Sources on the Net" collection. Mel Westerman, business librarian at Pennsylvania State University, had asked for volunteers from the Buslib-L discussion group to collect and annotate the resources in the many different subtopic areas of business. Hope Tillman, director of Babson College libraries, was one of the key volunteers. Leslie Haas volunteered to coordinate the volunteers and publish the list on the Internet. This list was then organized and published on the Kent State University Gopher server and FTP server, which are now defunct. With the advent of the Web, many of "Business Sources on the Net" volunteers and other business librarians began collecting Internet business information resources and organizing them on their own Websites. The Internet business resources identification and collection strategies that the original Buslib-L volunteers used involved monitoring and searching with some of the Internet resource collection tools described below.

Websites Which Review and Evaluate Internet Business Information Resources: Other E-libraries, Subject Collection Guides/Webliographies

Several business subject collections, metasites, and e-libraries are included in this chapter's Webliography. The most promising sites in terms of thorough annotations, evaluations, and scope of subject coverage are the Binghamton University Libraries–Business & Economics Resources (http://library.lib. binghamton.edu/subjects/business/basicbus.html) and Sheila Webber's Business Information Resources on the Internet (www.dis.strath.ac.uk/business/ index.html).

Discussion Lists and Newsgroups Where Individual Participants Review and Evaluate Internet Business Information Resources

The core discussion lists and newsgroups related to business Internet resources for business libraries is Buslib-L. Buslib-L is a moderated discussion list that addresses all issues relating to "the collection, storage, and dissemination of business information within a library setting—regardless of format." Subscription information and archives are available at www.willamette.edu/~gklein/ buslib.htm. Use the archives to search for information about individual Internet resources or subscribe for ongoing discussions. For example, search for "Thomas Register" to find out what Buslib-L subscribers think about *Thomas Register Online*. Other useful discussion groups for business Website reviews include SOHO-SPIDER, which discusses and reviews Websites for small-business related information. Use *The Directory of Scholarly and Professional Electronic Conferences* (through www.arl.org/scomm/edir/index.html) or The PHOAKS project (www.phoaks.com) to identify more discussion lists which review Internet business information sites.

E-journals and E-newsletters Which Publish Reviews and Evaluations of Internet Business Information Resources

Many of the business resource metasites included with this chapter also publish e-newsletter or e-journals as part of their basic service. The Dow Jones Business Directory (http://businessdirectory.dowjones.com/) and the Grail Search (www.grailsearch.com) sites both publish reviews of business-related Websites as well as organizing and linking to many sites. The Internet Scout Report project (http://scout.cs.wisc.edu/) also publishes an excellent e-newsletter, *The Scout Report for Business and Economics*, which distributes bi-weekly reviews of Internet resources of interest to researchers and educators in the business and economics fields. As discussed in Chapter One, additional e-journals and e-newsletters which review Internet business information resources may be identified by searching the NewJour archives (http://gort.ucsd.edu/newjour/) or the *ARL Directory of Electronic Journals Newsletters and Academic Discussion Lists* companion database Website (www.arl.org/scomm/edir/index.html).

Print Books and Journals Which Review Internet Business Information Resources

Several excellent books have been published recently which provide assistance in identifying good business information Websites. *Internet Resources and Services for International Business: A Global Guide* (1998) by L.G. Liu, reviews and annotates hundreds of international business-related Websites from over 17 countries. Two other books, *Essential Business Websites: You Need to Use Everyday* and *Essential Soho Websites: Small Office/Home Office Online Treasures*, are unpublished at this writing but the pre-publication descriptions indicate that these will be useful collection tools for Internet business e-libraries.

Most business journals and newsletters frequently include reviews of Internet resources either as articles or, in the same section, as book reviews. *Barrons, Inc., Fortune*, and *The Wall Street Journal* have featured Internet resource reviews in nearly every issue in the past year. Library-related serials including *Choice, Library Journal, College and Research Libraries, and American Libraries* also review Internet resources for business and other subjects in each issue. These were discussed in-depth in Chapter One.

Evaluating Internet Business Information Resources

Evaluating business information found on the Internet requires answers to the same basic questions that should be asked about any source of information. Business, medical, and legal information are especially sensitive. Quality of information on these subjects can affect the financial and physical well-being of library clients. Therefore, it is particularly important to very carefully evaluate any source of information in these subject areas. Evaluation of Internet health and medical information resources is discussed in Chapter Four. Evaluation of Internet legal information resources is discussed in Chapter Five. Business information may affect the financial success or failure of individuals, businesses, and organizations. It is therefore of great importance that it be accurate, timely, and secure. To evaluate Internet business information, use the basic Internet information resource evaluation strategies described in Chapter One. The emphasis with business information evaluation should be on the timeliness, security, and accuracy of the information.

Who Provided the Information? What is Their Reputation as an Information Provider?

The reputation of any provider of business information is very important in business decision making. Information obtained from Goldman-Sachs or Zacks, or another reputable brokerage, has more credibility than information obtained from "some guy" on a Usenet newsgroup or Web chat. The only way to determine the source of information provided on the Internet is to **read** through the Website, e-mail message, or newsgroup posting and look for an attribution. If you cannot easily determine who published business information, then it is best not to use it. Reputation of a business information source is usually based on their record of successful predictions and analyses.

Does the Business Information Provider Have the Authority or Expertise to Provide Information on That Topic?

In business, authority and expertise go hand in hand. Providers of business information are expected to have both education and experience in researching and analyzing financial, economic, and other business data. Education is not as important as experience and the information provider's record of successful predictions and analyses. Use the same strategy to find this information as you did in determining who provided the information. Again, if it is not clear to you that the information provider has the requisite experience and expertise, do not use the information.

Is the Information Provided for Current Information or for Historical Purposes? Does Currency or Lack of Currency Affect the Quality of the Information? When was the Last Update of the Information?

Much business information, especially financial information, needs to be as current as possible. Stock and commodities prices, currency exchange rates, news about current events which affects business, agriculture reports, and so on, are very time sensitive. Publication on the Internet, potentially, implies that this source of business information is the most current information available. Sites such as CNN Financial News (www.cnnfn.com) can provide all the types of information described above, and provide them with a date and time stamp so that the information user knows precisely the time at which the information was gathered and published. Other kinds of business information are actually historical in nature. Economic trends, changes in an industry over time, stock values over time, as well as changes in the products, personnel, and mission of individual companies are historical information. Look through Websites and e-serials to verify times and dates of publication. Use the strategies described in Chapter One if the information is not easily determined by reading through the Website or e-publication and the information seems valuable enough to make a further effort.

Is Security Important in Interacting with a Given Internet Business Information Source? Is a Site Likely to be Hacked and Information Altered? Will Personal or Financial Information be Requested From Clients?

Business information is an Internet subject area where security is extremely critical from both the site security and client security perspectives. These two security questions are very different. The information user needs to feel that the information that they are finding on the Internet has not been altered by an agent other than the original information provider. They also need to know that the Website in question is actually published by the organization it seems to be published by. See the discussion of Website hacking in Chapter One. In engaging in e-commerce, the client needs to feel secure in giving their personal and financial data to a company through their Internet presence. Personal and financial information should never be submitted over the Internet through un-encrypted e-mail or Web forms. Always use Web browser functionality to determine the security certification of any Website which requests personal or financial data be input.

Is Privacy of Internet-Business-Information-Seeking Behavior an Important Factor for You or Your Clients?

Some business research requires privacy in order to ensure information security. Industrial espionage is a very real problem in our modern global economy. If a competitor learns that a given company is researching along a certain line, that knowledge may give them a competitive advantage in developing or marketing a product, obtaining a contract, or recruiting desirable personnel. The fact that there is no privacy on the Internet may be a problem for many businesses. For example, a friend of mine used to be a librarian for a high-tech, research and development division of a Fortune 100 company. That friend would call me at my library and ask me to research certain things on the Internet rather than doing the research from their own Internet connection. That way it just looked like someone at Kent State University was researching in a particular area rather than someone in company *x*. Public libraries may find that business people are using their Internet services for the same reason. Researching from a public library Internet terminal is relatively anonymous. All the Website owners can find out is that someone at library *x* is researching a particular topic. Overall, this is a positive trend as it means librarians also have the opportunity to prove their value to the businesses in their communities. It also may result in increased research assistance to those businesses when they are using the library or need research done and faxed, e-mailed, or reported over the telephone.

Selecting a Core Internet Business Ready-reference Collection

As discussed in Chapter One, using an existing reference collection as a model is a good selection strategy. Figure 3.1 reports the core business reference tools listed by Libref-L and Publib subscribers. This model collection was used to choose Internet business ready-reference tools that closely map to the information content and quality of these traditional business reference tools. Notice that the types of reference resource identified in the collection plan are included. Additional selection criteria for business information resources can be derived from the answers arrived at during the collection planning process. The access, design, and content criteria for assessing the value of Websites for library users are reproduced in Table 3.1. The business Internet reference core collection included below was compiled with these criteria in mind. The intended client group is English-speaking adults who might be interested in basic business reference information regardless of their educational level. All

Figure 3.1   June 15, 1999 Report on Core Business Reference Tools Posted to Libref-L and Publib

Date: Tue, 15 Jun 1999 13:10:35 -0400
Subject: Survey Results: Core Reference Tools

===== Original Message From "Diane K. Kovacs" <diane@kovacs.com> =====

Thank you all very much to everyone who responded. Here are the core reference tools survey results from my previous question to this list (sorry for cross-posting inconveniences). They are in approximately order of their mention with some notes from me and comments from respondents. Please feel free to send me your core reference tools. I can always add to these. Thank you all again!

3. What are your two most used reference tools for business questions?

Southern California Business Directory—provides addresses, contact information, and some sales data for many local businesses. Main directory is by SIC (or whatever the new classification is called)/subject, with geographic, zip code, and alphabetical listings.
ValueLine Investment Survey
Duns Million Dollar Directory
American Business Disk
Dun and Bradstreets Business Directories
Hoover's directories
Standard & Poors Register
Thomas Register of American Manufacturers
Moody's Industrial Manual
Business InfoTrac Online
Directory of Corporate Affiliations
Illinois Services Directory
Infotrac Company Profiles
Morningstar Mutual Fund Survey
Poor's Company Directory
Wisconsin Business Services Directory (published by State Chamber of Commerce)
Wisconsin Manufacturers Directory Plus
California Manufacturers and Service Industry Directories
for Product Complaint—Gale's Brands and their companies

Table 3.1   Content Criteria for Internet Resources

Selection Adapted from Caywood (1996) (http://www6.pilot.infi.net/ ~carolyn/criteria.html)

1. Does the resource meet some current awareness related information need of the e-library's intended clients?
2. Does the resource provide the information at a level and language suitable to the age, educational background, and subject interests of the e-library's intended clients?
3. Does the resource provide information in a form that you want to include in your e-library? News services or e-serials, for example.

Other Selection Criteria Specific to Internet Resources Are:

4. Access and Design
   Will the e-library's intended clients have the computer equipment and software needed to use the resource? Does the resource allow for access by disabled individuals who may need to use text-to-voice software or other enabling tool? Does the resource display in the Web browser within a reasonable amount of time?

5. Archiving
   Will the information provider provide "back issues" or archives of the resource? Will you need to make arrangements to store such information locally if needed? This is especially important in the case of e-serials or current information that will become valuable historical information over time. Most social sciences research information will require some kind of archiving arrangements be made. It doesn't really matter if the information is archived in print publications, backed up to CD-ROM, magnetic tape or other electronic storage media, or simply kept available on the Web for an indeterminate period as long as researchers are assured that it will be archived and available in the future.

6. Cost/Licensing/User Access Control
   Some Internet accessible resources are fee-based. If that is the case, for example as with the *Encyclopedia Britannica* online, consideration will need to be made for not only the cost of the resource, but any licensing arrangements or user access control that must be exercised. For example, will the resource only be accessible by users from within the library's domain or can any library user from any location by using a login and password or library card number access the resource.

these core business reference Websites conform to international standards for Web browser compatibility, with no special software required for access. At least some information provided by each of these sites is free of direct cost. Many have additional special fee-based services such as document delivery or more advanced search options. Several require registration. The registration serves as a marketing research tool for the information provider. Many Websites are funded by advertising. The information provider uses the information obtained during the registration procedure to count their "circulation" demographics. This is the same principle used by newspapers and magazines. They sell advertising based on the circulation rate and demographics that they can guarantee to advertisers. However, registering on Websites may result in having your e-mail address included in junk e-mail lists. Most reputable sites provide an opportunity for you to opt out of such lists.

Business Core Internet Ready-reference Collection

Abstracts and Indexes

Bibliographies—See *Webliography of Business Metasites*

Dictionaries
OneLook Dictionaries, The Faster Finder
www.onelook.com/
The ultimate Internet dictionary lookup site. Search 475 general and specialized English dictionaries simultaneously, or select the ones you want to search. More than two million words now indexed.

Directories
Hoover's Online Business Directory
www.hoovers.com
Fee-based area available but the free information is equivalent and in some ways better than the print version of similar business directories.

Thomas Register
www.thomasregister.com

E-Serials
Forbes
www.forbes.com/
Full text of articles from *Forbes*, *Forbes FYI*, and *Forbes ASAP*. Searchable and updated daily.

Inc.
www.inc.com/
Full text of selected *Inc.* magazine stories. Monthly with archives.

Value Line Publishing
www.valueline.com/
Requires registration, but has many free articles and reports as well as research from the *Value Line* investment publications. Also provides subscription access to *Value Line* publications.

Encyclopedias
Information Please: Online Dictionary, Internet Encyclopedia, & Almanac Reference
www.infoplease.com/
Searchable collection of business and economics information from online almanacs, dictionaries, and the *5th Edition Columbia Encyclopedia* online.

Nolo's Legal Encyclopedia
www.nolo.com/briefs.html
Small business related legal information as well as 14 other categories of common-sense lanaguage legal information.

Key Primary Documents
   (Annual Reports, Law Codes, Statistical Sources, etc.)
Annual Reports/Company Web Pages Web100
www.metamoney.com/w100/
Lists the largest U.S. and international corporations on the Web today, along with hyperlinks to their sites.

CorpTech
www.corptech.com/
Premier site for research on America's technology manufacturers and developers; database of 50,000 high-tech companies.

Investor Communications Business, Inc.
www.icbinc.com/
Comprehensive source for annual reports; financial information available for over 3,500 U.S., Canadian, and U.K. companies.

GPO Access on the Web Full-text
www.access.gpo.gov
Searchable access to the Federal Register, Code of Federal Regulations, Congressional Documents, Directory and Index, the budget of the U.S. Govern-

ment, and more. Made available through the GPO Website (has the Code of Federal Regulations) or Purdue University Libraries.

Security and Exchange Commission (SEC) Edgar
www.sec.gov
Can be used to transmit a company filing (10K reports, etc.) as well as to search and retrieve them.

Internal Revenue Service
www.IRS.gov
Full-text publication, forms, and information for business taxes.

Stat-USA
www.stat-usa.gov
Fee-based access to current economic, financial, and other statistical documents provided by the U.S. Department of Commerce.

Uniform Commercial Code - Legal Information Institute - Cornell Law School
www.law.cornell.edu/uniform/ucc.html

News (Current Events)
CNN Financial News
www.cnnfn.com/
CNN financial network Website. Contains full-text of CNN's financial news stories and links to financial and other data.

Yahoo or *Excite*
http://quote.yahoo.com
www.excite.com
Current stock market quotes, currency and exchange information, and market and company analysis.

Wall Street Journal Interactive Edition
www.wsj.com/
Selected news from the *Wall Street Journal* updated hourly. Free trial full-text version but the full-text version is fee-based.

Table of Contents Services
UnCover
http://uncweb.carl.org/
Contents information of 18,000 journal titles including many business-related serials. There is free access to the UnCover database to look at citations. Image download, fax, or postal document delivery is fee-based.

The Internet Jobs and Employment Information Resource Collection Plan

What Purpose Will Your Web-based Jobs and Employment E-library Collection Serve? For Whom Are You Collecting Internet Jobs and Employment Resources?

There are two obvious purposes such an e-library collection might serve: access to job listings and application information for job seekers and information about career choices and vocational/educational preparation for different careers. School, academic, and public libraries are likely to need to provide e-library resources that support both purposes. Students eventually graduate and need to find jobs. A library client may be job seeking at any time. Furthermore, young people or individuals looking for a career change will find the information about career choices and vocational/educational preparation invaluable. Special business libraries are unlikely to want to collect resources for job-seekers. They may, however, support their personnel departments in recruiting employees by maintaining awareness of some of the sites where resumes are posted.

What Types of Jobs and Employment Internet Information Sources Will You Link to Through Your E-library?

Jobs and employment Internet information sources take forms that can be described in terms of traditional reference source types. An annotated "Jobs and Employment Core Internet Ready-Reference Collection" at the end of this section lists essential Internet reference tools organized by these reference source types.

1. Directories of occupational descriptions, employment sources, and vocational information.
2. Dictionaries of jobs and employment terminology.
3. Bibliographies of jobs-and-employment related information sources; see the Webliographies of Jobs and Employment Resource Metasites (at the end of this chapter).
4. Encyclopedias of occupational and employment information.
5. News and current awareness sources are the most important information sources for job seekers and employers. In this area the Internet supplies tools which are without peer in the print world. Some of the most global jobs and employment information and "want-ads" sites are listed in the core reference collection presented later in this section.

How Will You Organize Your Internet Jobs and Employment Resources?

Jobs and employment information can be organized by job type or subject area, depending on the nature of the collecting library.

Identifying and Collecting Internet Jobs and Employment Information Resources

Websites Which Review and Evaluate Internet Jobs and Employment Information Sources: Other E-libraries, Subject Collection Guides/Webliographies, Etc.

There is one guide to jobs and employment resources on the Internet that stands head and shoulders above any others: The Riley Guide: Employment Opportunities and Jobs Resource on the Internet (www.dbm.com/jobguide/). It is the ultimate source for these types of information on the Internet. For many libraries, providing a link to the Riley Guide and links to local jobs sites may be sufficient for their jobs and employment e-library collection.

Discussion Lists and Newsgroups Where Individual Participants Review and Evaluate Internet Jobs and Employment Resources

There is no single discussion list or newsgroup for all jobs and employment resource discussions. A number of discussion lists and newsgroups related to jobs and employment Internet resources for specific occupations can be found using *The Directory of Scholarly and Professional Electronic Conferences* (www.arl.org/scomm/edir/index.html*)* and The PHOAKS project (www.phoaks.com).

E-journals and Newsletters Which Publish Reviews and Evaluations of Internet Jobs and Employment Information Resources

The Scout Report (http://scout.cs.wisc.edu/index.html) frequently reviews Internet resources of interest to job-seekers and employers. Other e-serials which review Internet resources for job seekers in various professional capacities can be identified by searching the NewJour archives (http://gort.ucsd.edu/newjour/) or the *ARL Directory of Electronic Journals, Newsletters, and Academic Discussion Lists* companion database Website (www.arl.org/scomm/edir/index.html).

Print Books and Journals Which Review Internet Jobs and Employment Information Resources

Plunkett's Employers' Internet Sites With Careers Information (1999) profiles hundreds of Websites where major employers list job openings, salaries/benefits information, and provide opportunities to apply online. Marget Riley Dikel's *The Guide to Internet Job Searching : 1998–99* reviews the best Websites and strategies for job-seekers. One other book *Jobsearch.Net* (1998) guides readers through the process of researching jobs and employment information on the Internet.

Evaluating Internet Jobs and Employment Information Resources

Evaluation of jobs and employement information is highly idiosyncratic. One person's good job information is definitely not everyone's idea of good job information. Jobs and employment information needs to be accurate and current. The strategies for evaluating resources described in Chapter One work exceedingly well for jobs and employment information. It is very unlikely that a jobs and employment information Web page will not have an attribution and contact information. After all, how else will they expect the job-seeker to contact them and apply for their positions? In the case of general employment information, such as resume guides, employment outlook reports, cost-of-living, and salary surveys, the prime criteria must be the source of the data provided. For example, the *Occupational Outlook Handbook* is published by the U.S. Bureau of Labor Statistics based on data they have gathered from employers and other sources.

Selecting a Core Internet Jobs and Employment Ready-reference Collection

Selection criteria for Internet jobs and employment information resources are derived from the answers arrived at during the collection planning process. The core jobs and employment reference tools identified by Libref-l and Publib subscribers are reproduced in Figure 3.2. All of the reference tools included in this list are available on the Internet. The access, design, and content criteria for assessing the value of Websites for library users are reproduced in Table 3.1 presented earlier in this chapter. The Jobs and Employment Internet Ready-Reference Collection included below was compiled with these criteria in mind. This core Internet jobs and employment ready-reference collection is designed for English-speaking adults or students who might be interested in looking for a job or learning about employment opportunities. The educational level tends to be post-secondary because the jobs that are advertised on the Internet tend

---

**Figure 3.2   June 15, 1999 Report on Core Jobs and Employment
Reference Tools Posted to Libref-L and Publib**

5. What are your two most used reference tools for jobs and employment
   questions?

The number one source by a lot:
Occupational Outlook Handbook (comment: "Occupational Outlook Handbook is THE most frequently used source, nothing else really comes close")

Others:
Assortment of resume books kept at reference desk
Internet
Local newspaper help wanted ads
Career Information Center (13v., Macmillan Pub.)
Help Wanted USA (job ads from multiple Sunday papers on microfiche)
Infotrac Company Profiles
Directory of Executive Recruiters
Moody's Manuals (comment: "that huge news collection")
Career Information Center (Ferguson) or Encyclopedia of
   Careers and Vocational Guidance (Macmillan)
Ferguson's Encyclopedia of Careers and Vocational Guidance
American Almanac of Jobs and Salaries
Ohio Industrial Directory

---

to be professional or academic-level jobs. All Websites chosen for this collection conform to international standards for Web browser compatibility and
other design standards. Most of them are free for job-seekers. Several have
special fee-based services for employers or recruiters listing their positions.
Several require registration, but not a fee. The registration serves as a marketing research tool for the information provider as described in the previous
section.

Jobs and Employment Core Internet Ready-reference Collection

E-serials
Monthly Labor Review
http://stats.bls.gov/opub/mlr/mlrhome.htm
Publication of the United States federal government which reports employment trends and statistics.

News (Current Events)
America's Job Bank
www.ajb.dni.us/
Information from the U.S. Department of Labor for both job-seekers and employers; links to Talent Bank, Career Infonet, and Learning Exchange.

Career.com
www.career.com
Recruitment site featuring a real-time Cyberfair™—virtual job fair.

Monster.com
www.monster.com/
Job listings for seekers, create a resume, search companies, and information for recruiters.

NationJob
www.nationjob.com/
Comprehensive listings of jobs available by field/position, and/or location, and/or education. Profile and search for companies that meet your criteria.

USA Jobs (official U.S. federal jobs site)
www.usajobs.opm.gov/

Work Web
www.work-web.com
Input and retrieve information related to employment, training, education, and associated services

Key Primary Documents (annual reports, law codes, and statistical sources)
Homefair.com
www.homefair.com/
Salary calculator, moving calculator, and relocation information

Occupational Outlook Handbook
http://stats.bls.gov/opbhome.htm

E-library Builder Stories

Ohio Public Library Information Network (OPLIN) Website

www.oplin.lib.oh.us
Contact: Becky Wright, managing editor, wrightbe@oplin.lib.oh.us

The OPLIN e-library Website was created in furtherance of the OPLIN mission statement:

> The Mission of the Ohio Public Library Information Network (OPLIN) is to ensure equity of access to information for all Ohio citizens.
> The overriding rationale for OPLIN is to ensure that all citizens have equal access to information, regardless of location or format and regardless of location of the user.
> Equity of Access to information for all citizens must include:
> Access to the diverse resources of Ohio's public libraries.
> Access to federal, state, regional, and local information resources.
> Access to other electronic information resources.
> To achieve this Mission the Ohio Public Library Information Network will: D. Maintain and enhance an easy-to-use, front-end server to the variety of electronic information resources made available through OPLIN . . . Adopted March 14, 1997. (www.oplin.lib.oh.us/products/ABOUT/mission.html)

The OPLIN Website e-library was planned as a core OPLIN service from the very beginning of the OPLIN organization. The project was planned with the mission statement clearly in mind. The collection plan was developed by the original resource collectors and the OPLIN Board of Trustees:

> . . . they wrote an Electronic Resources Selection Policy Statement—adopted June 13, 1997—that governed and still governs selection of commercial and free-on-the-Web resources. (www.oplin.lib.oh.us/products/ABOUT/POLICIES/respol.html)

The OPLIN Website E-library is organized by general topic and subtopic areas. It includes access to fee-based databases, as well as to thousands of Web links in nearly two dozen topics and hundreds of subtopic areas. Because the OPLIN Website serves primarily the library patrons of the state of Ohio, there is a concentration on building the collection of Ohio-related information on the Web.

The Website and the OPLIN networking, hardware, and software set-up were outsourced to OARNET, the State of Ohio, and the State Library of Ohio's regional Internet provider. The Web server is UNIX-based.

The cost for the initial networking, Web server set-up, and Web hosting was relatively high because everything had to be purchased and set-up from scratch:

> The first year of the contract with our Web host was approximately $170,000. This covered equipment, software, programming, web hosting, and OARnet personnel.

Personnel costs for the creation of the e-library were not direct. A Webmaster, Daryl Weir, was made available full-time by the State Library of Ohio.

The on-loan Webmaster and OARnet personnel built the initial Web-based e-library on the OPLIN Website, including the popular Discover Ohio.

"The original resource collectors for the OPLIN Website were members of the Database Selection Committee and the OH! Kids Committee. These members were working librarians from around the state along with library specialists." A contractor, Gail Junion-Metz, was hired to work with OARnet personnel to create and maintain the children's area, OH! Kids.

Currently, the staff member at OPLIN designated to collect resources for all subject areas is Becky Wright, the managing editor. Her job is to design and write specifications for the Website, as well as to supervise both development and maintenance programming. In addition, she determines the look and feel of the site, the audience, and point of the site, and ensures that the information presented supports the directives and policies of the OPLIN Board of Trustees and the Executive Director.

Wright also adds new links and organizational structures to the Website on a daily basis. In order to do this effectively, she monitors daily news, current events, and issues of the day and attempts "to make the latest, most relevant Web information available quickly to reference librarians across the state through the OPLIN Website."

OPLIN networks with the people and organizations that it serves. The organization "pursues relationships with other state agencies to inform them of the free public Web access available to their constituents in every county and conducts joint promotions and other projects with them," as well as "partnerships with other organizations, such as Fannie Mae, to extend information to Ohio library patrons."

OPLIN must maintain relationships with database vendors and work with them to promote their services through the OPLINLIST discussion list and the OPLIN News posted on the site. OPLIN personnel also work with the libraries and the public to maintain links, add new ones, post relevant information, and verify accessibility.

OPLIN has recently begun hiring freelance, part-time contributing editors for specific topic areas. Several topic areas were targeted for special collection efforts as a result of surveys of Ohio public librarians. These contributing editors:

> . . . seek out high-quality Web links related to each subject specialty and add them directly to the OPLIN Website database via proprietary, Web-based administrative tools, write short articles discussing specific topics within their subject specialties, and keep the managing editor informed of any trends on the Web related to their subject areas.

The managing editor trains contributing editors to use the tools and supervises their work.

> The contributing editor program makes it possible to build up and monitor select content areas and keep them current much more efficiently by distributing the work to subject matter specialists. We have three CEs right now. . . . Diane K. Kovacs for business information, Danna Rubel for children's (OH! Kids), and Donovan Ackley for genealogy. We intend to hire three more during the first year of this Biennium . . . for the Discover Ohio, government & law, and young adult (OH! Teens) areas.

Marketing the Website to the libraries, library patrons, and government agencies in the state of Ohio is a major effort for the OPLIN Website managing editor and the executive director. They:

> make presentations to various interest groups around the state and distribute press releases to Ohio radio stations and local newspapers to promote local library use, free connectivity, and the availability of quality information on the Web.

The OPLIN Website e-library is a huge project with corresponding personnel requirements. Wright, the full-time managing editor, spends 80 percent of her time with ongoing development and maintenance of the OPLIN Website e-library. Contributing editors contribute 15–25 hours per month each.

> A designated "Webmaster" from the Web hosting contractor—35 percent (estimate) and programmers from the Web hosting contractor—time spent varies; assigned by project, so when the project is going on, it's 100 percent, but sometimes during the year it's just maintenance work and could be as little as 5–10 percent of their time.

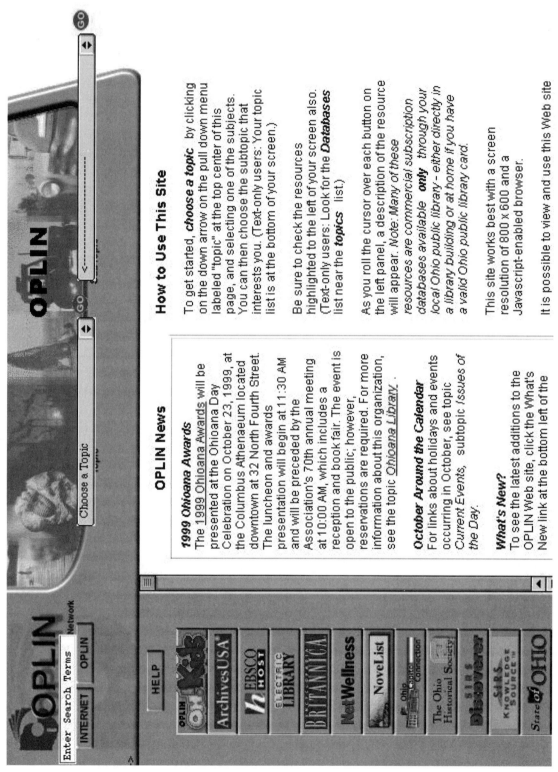

How to Use This Site

To get started, ***choose a topic*** by clicking on the down arrow on the pull down menu labeled "topic" at the top center of this page, and selecting one of the subjects. You can then choose the subtopic that interests you. (Text-only users: Your topic list is at the bottom of your screen.)

Be sure to check the resources highlighted to the left of your screen also. (Text-only users: Look for the ***Databases*** list near the ***topics*** list.)

As you roll the cursor over each button on the left panel, a description of the resource will appear. *Note: Many of these resources are commercial subscription databases available **only** through your local Ohio public library – either directly in a library building or at home if you have a valid Ohio public library card.*

This site works best with a screen resolution of 800 x 600 and a Javascript-enabled browser.

It is possible to view and use this Web site

OPLIN News

1999 Ohioana Awards
The 1999 Ohioana Awards will be presented at the Ohioana Day Celebration on October 23, 1999, at the Columbus Athenaeum located downtown at 32 North Fourth Street. The luncheon and awards presentation will begin at 11:30 AM and will be preceded by the Association's 70th annual meeting at 10:00 AM, which includes a reception and book fair. The event is open to the public; however, reservations are required. For more information about this organization, see the topic Ohioana Library .

October Around the Calendar
For links about holidays and events occurring in October, see topic *Current Events*, subtopic *Issues of the Day*.

What's New?
To see the latest additions to the OPLIN Web site, click the What's New link at the bottom left of the

Ohio Public Library Information Network (OPLIN)

The OPLIN Website e-library will continue to expand and improve in quality with the hiring of additional contributing editors. OPLIN personnel are working on increasing the awareness of the service and to respond to the changing needs of the information users in the state of Ohio and elsewhere.

Columbus Metropolitan Libraries System—Library Channel

Columbus, Ohio, USA
Contact: Beth Black
bblack@cml.lib.oh.us
(Library building access only)
(Library Channel producer vImpact homepage: www.vimpact.net/tlc/ tlcov.htm)

The Columbus Metropolitan Libraries (CML) System chose to use the Library Channel (TLC) software to create their e-library of Internet resources. TLC software was originally programmed in a cooperative effort between the Westerville, Ohio, Public Library and vImpact, the company selling the product.

The Library Channel e-library is only available on networked computers within the library system. Users may not connect to TLC from locations outside of the main or branch library buildings. CML has 21 branch locations in addition to the main library in downtown Columbus, Ohio. The access limitation is an aspect of the Library Channel software.

CML administrators and other staff members saw a demonstration of TLC and then chose the software because of features that allow libraries to restrict access to Internet sites selected by the library.

"We followed an already written collection plan, our collection development policy and our scope statements. We did create a short guide for issues unique to the Internet also," CML administrators and staff say.

The CML staff used their general collection plan in creating their e-library to provide user-friendly Internet resource access for their library clients.

> Our goal in providing TLC for our clients is to make the Internet less overwhelming and easier to use for both the novice and proficient Internet users . . . We see this as an extension of our collection; now not only do we select books, videos, and audio materials, we also select Internet sites.

The Library Channel uses a modified form of Internet Explorer as a browser and it runs under the Windows 95/98/NT operating systems.

CML's Internet e-library was built by existing personnel on both the technical support side and the librarian side. Initial cost for the time personnel spent collecting Internet sites for the initial e-library—CML refers to the individuals responsible for Internet site selection as "linkers"—was approximately $10,000. This does not include the cost of the technical support provided by their IS staff.

There was no formal training for linkers or technical staff. The technical staff worked with the vImpact programmers to setup and troubleshoot the software. A select group of librarians were given basic instruction, by a vImpact representative, on how to link and create categories. These librarians then taught each of the librarians and library assistants who were selecting sites.

> We also provided some selection guidelines to be used in addition to our current selection policy for all other materials. Mostly we had a lot of informal communication about how the software worked and about changes as they occurred. Most of the librarians at main library had attended basic Internet training the previous year.

CML has integrated the selection of Internet sites for the Library Channel e-library into the general collection development duties of approximately 84 staff members (librarians and library assistants). Some individuals act as the organizers and evaluators for particular subject areas.

Only one additional staff member, a LAN specialist, was hired to work on TLC, but not exclusively. No additional librarians were required for the project. Beth Black took on the coordination of the selection and public service aspects of the product as part of her job.

Black estimates that the linkers probably spend five to ten hours a week on some aspect of selection and organization of sites. She probably "spend about one third of my time on some aspect of TLC support, sometimes more, sometimes less. I don't know how much time the IS guys spend."

TLC linkers select and update new sites everyday. TLC is regularly updated and expanded twice per week. A TCL committee led by Black, and made up of representatives from each main library division and from a couple branches led by Black, works regularly to improve the subject structure, locate missing topics, and support the linkers as much as possible.

Future plans include upgrading the browser and to make some form of TLC available to clients outside of the branches and main libraries.

Print and Electronic Publications Cited or Consulted in Chapter Three

Bergman, Thomas P., et al. 1998. *The Business Student Writer's Manual and Guide to the Internet*. Upper Saddle River, N.J.: Prentice Hall.

Bolles, R. *What Color is Your Parachute the Net Guide*. www.jobhuntersbible.com.

Liu, L. G. 1998. *Internet Resources and Services for International Business: A Global Guide*. Phoenix, AZ: Oryx Press.

Plunkett, J. W. 1999. *Plunkett's Employers' Internet Sites With Careers Information: The Only Complete Guide to Careers Websites Operated by Major Employers*. Houston, TX: Plunkett Research Ltd.

Riley-Dikel, M., Roehm, F., and Oserman, St. *The Guide to Internet Job Searching: 1998–99* (Serial). Lincolnwood, IL: Vgm Career Horizons.

Straub. C. 1998. *Jobsearch.Net*. Menlo Park, CA: Crisp Publications.

U.S. Bureau of Labor Statistics. 1999. *Occupational Outlook Handbook*. Washington, D.C.: U.S. Department of Labor.

Williams, K. 1999. *Essential Business Websites : You Need to Use Everyday*. Manakin-Sabot, VA: Hope Springs Press.

Williams, K. 1999. *Essential Soho Websites : Small Office/Home Office Online Treasures*. Manakin-Sabot, VA: Hope Springs Press.

Webliographies Included with Chapter Three

Business Resource Metasites

All Business Network
www.all-biz.com
Links to business-related sites: news, company information, reference, employment opportunities, and more.

Argus Clearinghouse—Business
www.clearinghouse.net/cgi-bin/chadmin/viewcat/
Business__Employment?kywd++
Contact: clearinghouse@argus-inc.com.
Directory of evaluated and annotated resource guides and directories in various business-related subjects. Revision dates vary, but are clearly noted.

Binghamton University Libraries - Business & Economics Resources
http://library.lib.binghamton.edu/subjects/business/basicbus.html
Contact: chailey@binghamton.edu

Annotated and updated business resources of accounting & tax, economics, finance & investment, international business, management, marketing, and social science data (then subdivided). Includes an annotated gateway to online business resources.

Biz/ed
www.bized.ac.uk/
Contact: Andy Beharrell, bized-info@bris.ac.uk
Biz/ed is a dedicated business and economics education gateway for students, teachers and lecturers.

Business Information Resources on the Internet
www.dis.strath.ac.uk/business/index.html
Contact: Sheila Webber, sheila@dis.strath.ac.uk
Selective guide to Internet sites which contain quality general business information.

Business Resources on the Internet
www.bizlink.org
Contact: webmaster@plcmc.lib.nc.us
This Website contains links covering topics of business-career, starting a business, research, marketing, and books (annotated, but not comprehensive).

CEO Express
www.ceoexpress.com
Contact: webmaster@ceoexpress.com
Huge directories of business-related links of current business news (newspapers, magazines, etc.), business research (banking, finance, law, etc.), tools (reference, maps, etc.), business travel, and Internet business issues.

Directory Guide
www.directoryguide.com/
Contact: Mark Bozzini, CEO; info@submit-it.com
Business which has an extensive catalog of search engines and directories of 18 topics.

Dow Jones Business Directory
http://businessdirectory.dowjones.com/
Contact: Glenn Fannick, Senior Producer; glenn.fannick@dowjones.com
Dow Jones editors write reviews about high-quality Websites relating to 12 business categories "without bias and with brevity and insight."

Find Links
www.findlinks.com/
Contact: info@findlinks.com
Directories of links to industry-specific Websites. More industries being added.

Grail Search
www.grailsearch.com
Contact: mail@grail.net (to submit site); improve@grail.net (other)
Directory format of filtered, reliable Internet information (Websites, discussions, tools, etc.) relating to international business.

IOMA—Business Management Supersite
www.ioma.com/about/site.shtml
Contact: www.ioma.com/infodesk/
The Institute of Management and Administration offers huge business directory of 16 industry sectors (600 links)—some annotated, all dated. The Management Library offers directory of online articles from their newsletter.

KiwiClub Web
http://riskweb.bus.utexas.edu/
Contact: Richard MacMinn; richard.macminn@bus.utexas.edu
Metasite maintained by the University of Texas, Austin provides links to other parts of the Internet that serve financial market information.

Krislyn's Strictly Business Sites
www.krislyn.com/sites.html
Huge directory of business sites, from accounting to writing. All annotated.

Louisiana State University—Business
www.lib.lsu.edu/weblio.html#Business
Contact: eslib@indigo.lib.lsu.edu
Internet subject guide of databases and resources for business.

Nerdworld
www.nerdworld.com/users/dstein/nw9.html
Contact: nerds@nerdworld.com
Directory of annotated business-related resources.

Pronet—Global Interactive Business Centre
http://pronet.ca/
Contact: webmaster@Pronet.ca
Multilingual international business-only search engine.

San Bernardino County Library—Business Resources
www.co.san-bernardino.ca.us/library/business.htm#business
Contact: rwatts@lib.co.san-bernardino.ca.us
Metasite categorized into five areas of general business, small business, investment, international trade, and personal finance; links are annotated.

Small Business Administration
www.sba.gov
Provides financial, management, and technical assistance with programs, initiatives, and information to anyone wanting to know about small business.

Strategis
http://strategis.ic.gc.ca
Contact: http://strategis.ic.gc.ca/cgi-bin/feedback/feed.pl/engdoc/sitedoc.html
Canada's premier and comprehensive business Website: company directories, learning resources, economic, research, employment, and marketing resources. Many ways to navigate: by search, category, or geographical location.

U.S. Business Advisor
www.business.gov
Contact: usba@sba.gov
Just about any information that businesses need from the federal government can be found through this page. It includes access to the GovBot searchable database to more than 10,000 government documents.

Yahoo Business and *Yahoo Finance*
http://smallbusiness.yahoo.com/
http://quote.yahoo.com/
Contact: smallbusiness-feedback@yahoo-inc.com; finance-admin@yahoo inc.com.
Links to research, U.S. and World markets, financial news, editorials, marketing, etc.

Jobs and Employment Resource Metasites

The Riley Guide
www.dbm.com/jobguide
Contact: Margaret F. Dikel; www.dbm.com/jobsguide/mfdikel.html
This comprehensive guide is more than job listings. Provides links to specific occupation databases of job listings or use the new A-Z guide for specific career positions, fields, and locations.

See **Collection Development Related Discussion Groups, E-serials and Guides, Evaluation Guides, and Workshops** Webliography in Chapter Two for discussion lists, newsgroups, e-serials, and other resources cited in this chapter.

4
Collecting Web-based Health and Medicine Information Resources

MEDLINEplus is designed to assist you in locating appropriate, authoritative health information sources. To accomplish this, NLM creates and maintains Web pages that point to selected Websites. Our emphasis is on information available from NLM and NIH. We include links to searches of MEDLINE, our database that indexes medical literature, and to the many full-text publications produced by the NIH institutes. We organize the information to help you locate the specific information you need. The information includes sections on health topics, dictionaries and glossaries for finding definitions of medical terms, links to major associations and clearinghouses, publications and news items, directories of health professionals and health facilities, and libraries that provide health information services for the public.

MEDLINEplus is not a list of every Web page on health, but is a selected list of quality sources. From MEDLINEplus Selection Guidelines (http://medlineplus.nlm.nih.gov/medlineplus/criteria.html).

Health and Medicine Internet Resource Collection and Evaluation

Health and medicine resources on the Internet support the information needs of healthcare consumers, healthcare providers, and medical researchers. The Internet has proven to be a convenient way to deliver health and medicine information to both consumers and healthcare providers. The public has begun to expect to find quality in-depth health and medicine information on the Web. Consumer and healthcare-provider-oriented metasites, such as Dr. Koop's Community (www.drkoop.com/), OnHealth.com (http://onhealth.com/), and WebMD (www.webmd.com/), are advertising their services and URLs during national television and radio programming. These metasites include original publications on a variety of health topics, searchable medical encyclopedias, dictionaries, and pharmaceuticals information, as well as collections of links to other health and medicine information Websites.

The Internet health and medicine resources available range from basic diagnostic and support information about diseases to pharmaceuticals and treatments for consumers, to continuing medical education and research information for healthcare providers.

The Internet Health and Medicine Information Resource Collection Plan

What Purpose Will Your Web-based Health and Medicine E-library Collection Serve? For Whom Are You Collecting Internet Health and Medicine Resources?

An e-library developed for a medical school library might support medical education for physicians, nurses, and other healthcare practitioners. Medical researchers will also find valuable Internet materials that assist in the dissemination and accumulation of medical research knowledge. The real value in Internet access to health and medicine information is for the practicing healthcare practitioner and for the healthcare consumer because it is available at the desktop. Hospital and clinic libraries will find plenty of valuable information to make available to their staff and patients. Public libraries and academic libraries might collect information intended for healthcare consumers.

What Internet Health and Medicine Information Resources Will You Link to Through Your E-library?

Internet health and medicine information resources take forms that can be described in terms of traditional reference source types. An annotated "Health and Medicine Core Internet Ready-Reference Collection" at the end of this section lists essential Internet health and medicine reference tools organized by these reference source types:

1. Directories of health and medicine information, such as hospital and healthcare-provider contact and statistical information.
2. Medical dictionaries.
3. Abstracts, indexes, and table of contents services for health and medicine serials such as PubMed and other Internet versions of the Medline database. The UnCover database is the original TOC service on the Internet and does provide TOC access to hundreds of health- and medicine-related serials. Many of the medical metasites also provide some indexing and/or abstracting, table of contents services, and some full-text access to print and medical e-serials.
4. Encyclopedias of health and medical information.*
5. Medical e-serials and full-text databases.
6. Bibliographies of health and medicine information resources (see the Medical and Health Metasites Webliography at the end of this chapter).*

7. Medical news.
8. Key primary documents such as medical and pharmaceutical research data.

*Health and medicine metasites often include all of these reference resource types in a single Website. In the case of the health and medicine metasites Webliography, those tools may also be used for health and medicine reference as well as to identify other Internet resources to collect.

How Will You Organize Your Internet Health and Medicine Information Resources?

Some consideration might be made for dividing Internet resources intended for healthcare providers from those intended for healthcare consumers. Health and medicine information can be organized by disease or treatment, or other formal structure such as the MeSH® medical subject headings used by the National Library of Medicine for its health and medical information products (www.nlm.nih.gov/mesh/).

Identifying and Collecting Internet Health and Medicine Information Resources

Websites Which Review and Evaluate Internet Health and Medicine Information Resources: Other E-libraries, Subject Collection Guides/Webliographies, Etc.

Several health and medicine subject collections, metasites, and e-libraries are included in this chapter's Webliography. The most promising sites in terms of annotations, evaluations, and scope of subject coverage are Anne Marie Malley's Biomedical and Life Sciences Site (www.calacademy.org/research/library/biodiv/biblio/sla98.htm) and the Hardin Meta Directory (www.lib.uiowa.edu/hardin/md/index.html).

Discussion Lists and Newsgroups Where Individual Participants Review and Evaluate Internet Health and Medicine Information Resources

The core discussion related to health and medicine Internet resources for libraries is MEDLIB-L, the Medical Libraries Discussion List. Another valuable health resource discussion list is HMATRIX-L, which focuses entirely on health and medical resources on the Internet. Example discussion lists which review medical specialty Websites include PSYCHIATRY-RESOURCES and ACCRI-L. The former discusses reviews of psychiatric information resource on the

Internet and the latter discusses reviews of anesthesia and critical-care information resources on the Internet. There are also literally hundreds of discussion groups for patient and family support. Use *The Directory of Scholarly and Professional Electronic Conferences* (through www.arl.org/scomm/edir) or The PHOAKS project (www.phoaks.com) to identify more health and medical discussion lists.

E-journals and E-newsletters Which Publish Reviews and Evaluations of Internet Health and Medicine Information Resources

One good example of this kind of tool is *Cancerwire* at www.rwneill.com/publishing/. *Cancerwire* is an e-newsletter which publishes general cancer news, clinical trials, support groups, Internet resource reviews, and other information for cancer patients, caregivers, and medical professionals. Hundreds of other e-serials which review Internet resources specific to hundreds of diseases and treatments and intended for healthcare consumers or healthcare practitioners can be found by searching the NewJour archives (http://gort.ucsd.edu/newjour/) or the *ARL Directory of Electronic Journals, Newsletters, and Academic Discussion Lists* companion database Website (www.arl.org).

Print Books and Journals Which Review Internet Health and Medicine Information Resources

A new book called *The Doctor's Always In: A Guide to + Best Health & Medical Information Sites on the Internet* (1999) by Schneider and Lidsky is very well organized with 25 chapters arranged by body system and specific disease categories. The annotations include the Website URL, a layperson's description of the information at that site, and, if available, the e-mail address of a contact person.

Several other books which review health and medicine Websites are included in the "Print and Electronic Publications Cited in this Chapter" section at the end of this chapter. Most of these, however, are out-of-date due to the rapid changes in the technology and health and medical culture of the Internet.

Medicine on the Net (COR Healthcare) is a new journal devoted to articles and features about health and medicine resources on the Internet. It provides a table of contents and subscription information at www.mednet-i.com/. Many mainstream medical journals including *JAMA* and *The New England Journal of Medicine* review health and medicine Internet resources. Popular family magazines such as *Women's Day* or *Family Circle* have featured reviews or articles about useful Websites for family health issues. These may be found by doing a *Reader's Guide to Periodical Literature*, *Infotrak*, or *Magazine Index* search in the print, CD-ROM, or online database version of these indexes. Library-related serials including *Choice, Library Journal, College and Research Libraries, American Libraries*, and so on also review Internet resources for health and medicine and other subjects in each issue. These serials were discussed in-depth in Chapter One.

Evaluating Internet Health and Medicine Information Resources

Kim et al. (1999) reviewed the published criteria for specifically evaluating health-related information on the Web. They found significant consensus on the key criteria for evaluating health and medicine Websites. The most frequently identified criteria were content quality, authority and disclosure of information source, currency of information, and accessibility of the Website.

Although evaluating health and medical information found on the Internet requires answers to the same basic questions as any other kind of information in selecting health and medical resources, quality must be a major criteria. Health and medical information quality may affect the life, health, and safety of human beings. It is therefore of great importance that it be extremely accurate and complete, or refer the healthcare consumer or provider to more in-depth information sources—or to advise them to consult a specialist. Library staff should not even give the appearance of providing health or medical advice to library clients. They must, however, be knowledgeable enough to select the very highest quality resources to provide to their clients. E-library resource collectors should evaluate each possible selection very carefully using the criteria described in Chapter One.

Who Provided the Information? What is Their Reputation as an Information Provider? Does the Information Provider Have the Authority or Expertise to Provide Information on That Topic?

When evaluating Internet health and medicine information these three questions should be answered at the same time. If an Internet health and medicine information resource has no provider attribution which includes the information provider's qualifications and background, it is unusable in a library, educational, clinical, or research setting. The metasites Dr. Koop's Community (www.drkoop.com/) and Medical Matrix (www.medmatrix.org/) illustrate good examples of the attribution information to expect from quality health and medicine information Websites. Dr. Koop's Community is intended for healthcare consumers and includes medical encyclopedia type information, pharmaceuticals information, e-serial publication of health- and medicine-related articles, as well as links to other health and medicine Internet resources.

Medical Matrix is intended for healthcare practitioners. Medical Matrix describes itself as containing links to "Ranked, peer-reviewed, annotated, updated clinical medicine resources."

Connect to Dr. Koop's Community and read through the page to look for the link "About Us." Read through the entire page, but pay special attention to the information linked to "Authors and Experts" and "Medical Advisory Board." Notice that these individuals are all healthcare professionals or medical educators. Notice also that their educational qualifications and professional and biographical information are provided.

Connect to Medical Matrix and login. Notice that the registration process implies that the site is intended for healthcare providers, medical practitioners, or librarians. Scroll down the screen until you see the links for "Inside Medical Matrix." These links provide details about the criteria for evaluation and selection of the resources included in the metasite:

> The Medical Matrix Project is devoted to posting, annotating, and continuously updating "full content, unrestricted access, Internet clinical medicine resources." Our target audience is primarily United States physicians and healthworkers who are on the front line in prescribing treatment for disease conditions.
>
> Medical Matrix assigns ranks to Internet resources based on their utility for point-of-care clinical application. Quality, peer review, full content, multimedia features, and unrestricted access are emphasized in the rankings. To ensure that the ranks are applied systematically and as objectively as possible, they are reviewed by our editorial board and assigned 1–5 stars according to the following guidelines. . . .

The "Meet our Editorial Board" link displays the names, qualifications, and links to professional and biographical information about the healthcare professionals and medical educators who perform the evaluation and selection of the resources included in the metasite. For example, one of the editors is listed:

> Neil B. Mehta, MD
> Department of General Internal Medicine—www.ccf.org/gim/—and
>   Division of Education—www.ccf.org/gim/cme/—Cleveland Clinic
>   Foundation;
> Clinical Assistant Professor of Medicine, College of Medicine of the
>   Pennsylvania State University;
> Associate Editor, Cleveland Clinic Journal of Medicine—
>   www.ccjm.org/

Notice that, further down the page, the contributors listed are all medical librarians!

Is the Information Provided for Current Information or for Historical Purposes? Does Currency or Lack of Currency Affect the Quality of the Information? When was the Last Update of the Information?

These questions should be very easily answered on a quality health and medicine Website. Although some sites do provide history of medicine materials, most sites try to provide current medical information. Verifying the dates and currency of a site can be critical to the healthcare consumer or healthcare practitioner using the information from the site to make a medical decision. For example, if the newest research shows that the best breast cancer treatment involves lumpectomy, radiation, and chemo—rather than mastectomy— it is important for both patient and surgeon to have that most current research result. Another recent case in point is the discovery of serious liver damage caused by the antibiotic "Trovan." A healthcare professional must have the very latest information about a drug in order to prescribe it safely. Using WebMD (www.webmd.com/) which was created for healthcare providers, search for information on the drug "Trovan." Do the articles discuss the liver damage side effect? What are the dates of the articles? Try this test with some of the other health and medicine resources listed in the Health and Medicine Core Internet Ready-Reference Collection and the Webliography provided in this chapter.

Is Security Important in Interacting with a Given Internet Information Source? Is a Site Likely to be Hacked and Information Altered? Will Personal or Financial Information be Requested From Clients?

Security is essential to ensure high-quality health and medicine information from the Internet. It is difficult to verify that security measures are in place without contacting the Website owners directly and asking them.

It is unlikely that clients will be asked for their financial information when accessing a health and medicine information site—unless it is also a storefront. It is possible to purchase herbs, health devices, alternative medical treatments, and dietary supplements through the Internet. Always look for a secure server before you input financial information. Use the strategies discussed in Chapter One.

It is more likely that clients will be asked for personal information when they access a health and medicine Website. For example, when you register for Medical Matrix you must provide your name, profession, and other personal data.

Is Privacy-of-Information-Seeking Behavior an Important Factor for You or Your Clients?

This is frequently an important factor for clients who are suffering from diseases, such as AIDS, that might inspire others to persecute or fear them, or genetic disorders that might cause insurance companies to no longer cover them. Great care should be taken, if possible, to warn clients that personal information is not private on the Internet.

Selecting a Core Internet Health and Medicine Ready-reference Collection

Selection criteria for any format in which you find health and medical information resources are derived from the answers arrived at during the collection-planning process. The Publib and Libref-L subscribers shared their core health and medicine reference tools and these are reproduced in Figure 4.1. Most of these reference tools have Internet counterparts. In at least one case, *The Physicians Desk Reference* (PDR), there is nothing currently on the Internet to match the quality and depth of coverage of the print *PDR*. There are some pharmaceutical information sites and metasites with drug databases that come close. It is possible to use this core health and medicine ready-reference collection as a model for selecting Internet health and medicine ready-reference resources. The access, design, and content criteria for assessing the value of Websites for library users are reproduced in Table 4.1. The health and medicine Internet ready-reference core collection included below was compiled with these criteria in mind. The intended client groups are English-speaking healthcare consumers and professionals. These clients might want either ready-reference type consumer health or medical information, or more in-depth, diagnostic, pharmaceutical and treatment information on a quick-response basis. The access and design of all these core Internet reference sources are based on standards of simplicity, international Internet Web browser compatibility, and no special software required for access. Most of them are free of direct cost—free except for the cost of Internet access—with some having special fee-based services including document delivery. Archiving of most critical information at these sites is assured by the publishers who provided the information in both print and other electronic storage media.

Table 4.1   Content Criteria for Internet Resources

Selection Adapted from Caywood (1996) (http://www6.pilot.infi.net/ ~carolyn/criteria.html)

1. Does the resource meet some current awareness related information need of the e-library's intended clients?
2. Does the resource provide the information at a level and language suitable to the age, educational background, and subject interests of the e-library's intended clients?
3. Does the resource provide information in a form that you want to include in your e-library? News services or e-serials, for example.

Other Selection Criteria Specific to Internet Resources Are:

4. Access and Design
   Will the e-library's intended clients have the computer equipment and software needed to use the resource? Does the resource allow for access by disabled individuals who may need to use text-to-voice software or other enabling tool? Does the resource display in the Web browser within a reasonable amount of time?
5. Archiving
   Will the information provider provide "back issues" or archives of the resource? Will you need to make arrangements to store such information locally if needed? This is especially important in the case of e-serials or current information that will become valuable historical information over time. Most social sciences research information will require some kind of archiving arrangements be made. It doesn't really matter if the information is archived in print publications, backed up to CD-ROM, magnetic tape or other electronic storage media, or simply kept available on the Web for an indeterminate period as long as researchers are assured that it will be archived and available in the future.
6. Cost/Licensing/User Access Control
   Some Internet accessible resources are fee-based. If that is the case, for example as with the *Encyclopedia Britannica* online, consideration will need to be made for not only the cost of the resource, but any licensing arrangements or user access control that must be exercised. For example, will the resource only be accessible by users from within the library's domain or can any library user from any location by using a login and password or library card number access the resource.

Figure 4.1 June 15, 1999 Report on Core Medical Reference Tools Posted to Libref-L and Publib

Date: Tue, 15 Jun 1999 13:10:35 -0400
Subject: Survey Results: Core Reference Tools

===== Original Message From "Diane K. Kovacs" <diane@kovacs.com> =====

Thank you all very much to everyone who responded. Here are the core reference tools survey results from my previous question to this list (sorry for cross-posting inconveniences). They are in approximately order of their mention with some notes from me and comments from respondents. Please feel free to send me your core reference tools. I can always add to these. Thank you all again!

4. What are your two most used reference tools for medical questions?

Merck Manual
PDR
Health Reference InfoTrac
Encyclopedia of Diseases (Springhouse?)
Consumer Reports Complete Drug Reference
Harrison's Principles of Internal Medicine
Pharmacopeia
Stedman's Medical Dictionary

Health and Medicine Core Internet Ready-reference Collection

Directories

American Hospital Directory

www.ahd.com/

This directory provides online, comparative data for most hospitals. Locate a hospital, obtain summaries, and other services. Subscribe for detailed information.

HealthNet

www3.uchc.edu/~uchclib/departm/hnet/

This site was developed to "assist in the development of local public libraries as primary access points for consumer health information."

Mayo Clinic Health Oasis

www.mayohealth.org/

This directory has nine information centers, headlines, articles, library, and "Ask Mayo" feature.

Searching In Health and Medicine

www.sc.edu/bck2skol/fall/health.html

This Website lists sites in various medical fields.

WellnessWeb

www.wellweb.com/

A comprehensive patient resource for alternative medicine, conventional medicine and nutrition/fitness.

Dictionaries

Antimicrobial Use Guidelines - Hypertext Antibiotic Guide

www.medsch.wisc.edu/clinsci/amcg/amcg.html

Search this guide: alphabetically by drug, by organism, by empiric therapy, by site, or by antimicrobial treatment of HIV infected patient.

OneLook Dictionaries, The Faster Finder

www.onelook.com/

The ultimate Internet dictionary lookup site. Search 475 general and specialized English dictionaries simultaneously, or select the ones you want to search. More than two million words now indexed.—[Annotation from LII]

Bibliographies—See *Webliography of the Health and Medicine Metasites*
Abstracts, indexes, and table of contents services—
See the *Webliography of Health and Medicine Metasites*

Medscape
www.medscape.com/
Searchable full-text of articles from a variety of medical journals and medical news publications. Requires registration, but is mainly free access with links to the medical journals in Dow Jones Interactive Publications Library on a pay-per-view basis. This site also includes published practice/clinical guidelines, a physicians-only discussion area, treatment updates, conference summaries and schedules, as well as a collection of patient resources sites.

UnCover
http://uncweb.carl.org/
Contents information of medical- and health-related journals.

Encyclopedias—
See the *Webliography of Health and Medicine Metasites*
See Medscape, above.

The Merck Manual of Diagnosis and Therapy 17th Ed. Online version
www.merck.com/pubs/mmanual-home

● ●

E-library Builder Story

San Bernardino Web E-library

> San Bernardino County Library, San Bernardino, California, USA
> www.co.san-bernardino.ca.us/library/
> Contact: Richard Watts
> rwatts@lib.co.san-bernardino.ca.us

The San Bernardino County Library's e-library Website was conceived by County Librarian Ed Kieczykowski as a way to provide selected library services to a large community of users. Kieczykowski says:

> San Bernardino County is the largest county in the contiguous United States, covering 20,131 square miles (51,961 square kilometers). About 90 percent of the county is desert; the remainder consists of the San Bernardino Valley, lying on the eastern outskirts of metropolitan Los Angeles, and the San Bernardino Mountains, a popular

resort area. The 1990 Census population was 1,418,380; the 1994 estimate was 1,591,800. The San Bernardino County Library serves a population of approximately one million through 27 branches and an administrative headquarters. Six cities in the county support autonomous city library systems.

The size of the county, and the resulting great distances between many isolated communities, creates unique telecommunications challenges for the county government. The county's Information Services Dept. has created an extensive telecommunications infrastructure, centered around a countywide Wide Area Network (WAN). When the WAN was established, the county established its own Internet domain, and offered Web space to all county departments.

Richard Watts, Coordinator of Technical Services, took the lead role in developing the Website. The current e-library includes such information about library policies, addresses, and hours, as well as a list of Internet resources. The site also includes an interactive reference question form and a weekly list of new titles. The interactive reference form was developed, and responses coordinated, through Reference Librarian Nannette Bricker-Barrett. Youth Services Coordinator Susan Erickson and her assistant Kristin Lane provide input for the youth services section. Dave Coleman, a library assistant at the Chino Hills branch, developed a branch homepage for his branch with financial support from the Friends of the Library. At this time the library is unable to provide access to their Online Public Access Catalog (OPAC) because of their internal network firewall, but plan to do so in the future.

Although the San Bernardino County librarians did not develop a written collection plan, they used their print general informational brochure as a guide for format and content. Some key features which were designed specifically for their community are neighborhood street maps, access to the PACs of neighboring public and academic libraries, and a useful list of Internet resources. Their collection of Internet resources is aimed at two audiences:

> . . . users outside the confines of the library who want a varied, current, substantial, and useful list of resources, many with a local emphasis; and library staff, many of whom are paraprofessionals, needing to help patrons in the branches with reference questions.

They began their collection process by incorporating the Internet resources selected by a nearby library's e-library collection compiled by Norm Reeder at the Torrance, California, Public Library. San Bernardino County librarians, primarily Watts, perform ongoing selection of Internet resources. Although he initially used resources compiled by other libraries, Watts now relies on published recommendation from established sources, principally *The Scout*

Report, the Librarians' Index to the Internet (www.lii.org), and *Library Journal*.

"Our goal is to inform the public about library policies, services, locations, etc., and establish a solid presence on the Web in anticipation of making our PAC available in the foreseeable future," Watts says. San Bernardino County considered creating a telnet-accessible version of their PAC rather than a Website:

> ... but telephone costs were a major obstacle. Our service area has two area codes, three telephone companies, and covers more than 20,000 square miles. Patrons in outlying areas would incur significant toll charges unless we established multiple telephone hubs or a costly toll-free service. The establishment of the county's WAN and Internet domain presented an ideal solution to these problems.

The Web server is run by county Information Services. Librarians use Internet connected PCs to revise and update the e-library Website.

Watts initially used Brooklyn North's freeware version of HTML Assistant, and later acquired the full commercial professional version. He eventually moved to a Compaq Pentium Deskpro running Windows 95, and uses Symantec's Visual Page to edit page content. He has both Netscape and Internet Explorer on the machine. Information Services used a variety of mapping software to create the initial branch neighborhood maps. Watts has revised some of the maps, and created new regional maps, using ESRI's Education Map Pro. ESRI, the leading geographic information systems company in the software industry, has its headquarters in Redlands, located in San Bernardino County. DRA's Report Writer, running on a VAX Alpha, is used to create a weekly list of new titles, broken down by MARC fixed-field material types and intellectual levels. He has also used some Java freeware downloaded from the Web. The online reference page was developed by Information Services using Javascript and Microsoft Active Pages. Watts validates his HTML markup using the Website "Dr. HTML" at (www.webreference.com/js/). PhotoShop, installed on a PC in another department, has been used to create graphics for the new homepage format introduced in the early summer of 1998. This format includes the use of frames and what is believed to be a more visually-pleasing font and background.

County Information Services edited and mounted the start-up version of the site as part the initial installation of the WAN and County Internet domain. These costs were included in ongoing interdepartmental overhead fees paid by the Library to Information Services.

Initially, Watts told county Information Services what was wanted, and they created the first Web page and the first neighborhood maps. The first revisions and updates were e-mailed to Information Services. After he became comfortable with HTML page markup, Watts was able to FTP new and revised pages to the county server using the freeware version of the program WS_FTP Pro.

Watts devoted a large amount of time to the project during its developmental phases, up to one half of his time. His ongoing commitment is estimated at one-quarter to one-third of his time spent revising and updating the Internet links [and the new Amazon.com links]. His training included a one-day course in HTML and Java from the University of California, Riverside extension service, and a "Friday Forum" on PhotoShop at UCLA's Graduate School of Education & Information Services. He studied a variety of materials from books, periodicals, and online tutorials. Coleman at the Chino Hills branch was largely self-taught. A large number of Information Services personnel maintain the county Internet domain and WAN on a 24/7 basis, with the library as a fairly minor component of the overall operation.

Their major future project for the e-library Website is to mount DRA's Web-based OPAC module, Web2\TAOS. There are a variety of financial obstacles involving hardware placed outside the county's firewall and DRA license fees.

The library became an Amazon.com Associate in August 1998. The library receives a small commission for sales initiated and completed through its homepage. The commission is larger if a library-recommended title is chosen. Suggestions include the "1998 Notable Children's Books" and "1998 Best Books for Young Adults" chosen by ALA, recent juvenile titles selected by the Youth Services Department, *Publisher's Weekly* best sellers, and "Oprah's Book Club" selections for adults. The latter two categories include book cover graphics provided by Amazon.com. Watts shrinks these graphics using Paint Shop Pro from Jasc Software.

> Research Pathfinders, created by Youth Services personnel in the branches, were added in October 1998. The topics covered include many used for high school and community college research papers, such as child abuse and genetic engineering. Pathfinders include related LC subject headings, standard reference books, Information Access and Reader's Guide subject headings, and Internet sites.

San Bernardino County Library

Selected Internet Resources

Area Library Catalogs

Catalog of Federal Government Documents

Quick Reference Sources

Area Study and Ethnic Resources

Business Resources (General Business, Small Business, Investment Resources, International Trade, Personal Finance)

Career Resources (Career & Employment Planning, Computer Magazines, Computer Manufacturers, Internet & World Wide Web, Operating Systems, Apples & Macs, MS-DOS/Windows PCs, Recycling Used Computers, Telecommunications, Viruses & Hackers, Year 2000 Problem)

Computer Resources (General Information, Specific Types of Careers, Small Business Information)

Education Resources (General Information, Grade K-8 Resources, Grade 9-12 Resources, Higher Education Resources, Finance, Scholarship & Grant Resources)

Entertainment and Sports Resources (Motion Pictures, Theater, Radio and Television, Music and Visual Arts, Sports)

Family and Social Issue Resources (Adoption, Family, Genealogy, Marriage & Divorce, Men & Women, Safety, Seniors, Social Action & Volunteerism, Youth)

Health Resources (General Information, Search Engines, Organizations, Specific Conditions)

History Resources

Kids and Teens (Research Pathfinders for use in San Bernardino County Branch Libraries, Fun Sites, Homework Help, Surf Lists of Youth Sites, Useful Sites for Parents & Teachers, Science Exploration)

Legal Resources

Library, Book and Author Resources (Libraries, Books, Authors and Literary Genres, Children's Literature, Poetry, Web Style)

News Resources

San Bernardino Web E-library

Print and Electronic Publications Cited or Consulted in Chapter Four

Davis, J. B., ed. 1998. *Health and Medicine on the Internet*. Los Angeles: Health Information Press.

Griffin D. 1998. Directory of Internet Sources for Health Professionals. Delmar Publications.

Kim, P., Eng, T. R., Deering, M.J., and Maxfield, A. (1999). "Published Criteria for Evaluating Health Related Websites: Review." *British Medical Journal* 318, No. 7184 (March 6, 1999):647. (www.bmj.com/cgi/content/full/318/7184/647).

Kovacs, Diane K. and Carlson, Ann L. 1999. *Health and Medicine on the Internet*. Berkeley: Library Solutions Press.

Logan, J. C. 1998. *Winning Websites for Medical Personnel and Patients*. Lemon Grove, CA: Lavida Books & Software.

Mathias, J. H. 1998. "Creation of a Web List for Clinical Disciplines." *College and Research Libraries News* v.59 no 10 (Nov. 98) 768–771.

Morrison, M. R. 1998. *Dsm-IV Internet Companion*. New York: W. W. Norton & Company.

Nicoll, L.H. 1998. *Computers in Nursing's Nurses' Guide to the Internet*. New York: Lippincott-Raven Publishers.

Schneider, J. S. and Lidsky, T. I. 1999. *The Doctor's Always In : A Guide to + Best Health & Medical Information Sites on the Internet*. Cherry Hill, NJ: Neuroinformatics, Inc.

Sharp, R. M. and Sharp V. F. 1998. *Webdoctor : Finding the Best Healthcare Online (Quality Medical Home Health Library)*. New York, New York: St. Martins Press, Griffin Trade Paperback.

Webliographies Included with Chapter Four

Medical and Health Resource Metasites

Achoo
www.achoo.com

American Medical Association
www.ama-assn.org
Doctor finder, peer-reviewed articles and publications, health information for both patients and physicians, and FREIDA (Fellowship and Resident Electronic Interactive Database).

Anne Marie Malley's BioMedical and Life Sciences Site
(www.calacademy.org/research/library/biodiv/biblio/sla98.htm)

Barnes Learning Resource Center
www.galter.nwu.edu/libinfo/lrc
Contact: galter-lrc@nwu.edu
Core databases generally relating to health sciences.

Biomedical and Life Sciences Sites
www.calacademy.org/research/library/biodiv/biblio/sla98.htm
Contact: Anne Marie Malley, amalley@calacademy.org
Large, well-organized, and easy-to-use database of annotated and reviewed sites.

Center For Disease Control and Prevention
www.cdc.gov
Contact: www.cdc.gov/netinfo.htm
Creates policy for public health; *EID (Emerging Infectious Diseases) Journal*; travel health, data and statistics; health information; links to other federal, non-federal, state and local health sites.

Comparison of Health Information Megasites
www.lib.umich.edu/megasite/
Contact: Pat Anderson, pfa@nwu.edu
Just a Web page with graphics that link to medical databases; identified as "the most useful sites for assisting with health sciences reference."

Dr. Koop's Community
(www.drkoop.com)

Doctors Guide to the Internet
www.pslgroup.com/docguide.htm
Contact: Webmaster@pslgroup.com
Easy-to-navigate site with annotated links to various medical and professional sites.

Hardin Meta Directory
www.lib.uiowa.edu/hardin/md/index.html
Contact: hardin-webmaster@uiowa.edu
Database of Websites by category, size of site, and connection rate is annotated. Also lists the Medical/Health Sciences Libraries on the Web.

HealthWeb
http://healthweb.org
Contact: healthweb@umich.edu

This site provides links to specific, evaluated information resources on the World Wide Web selected by librarians and information professionals at leading academic medical centers in the Midwest. Selection emphasizes quality information aimed at assisting healthcare professionals as well as consumers in meeting their health information needs.

Internet GratefulMed
http://igm.nlm.nih.gov/
Contact: access@nlm.nih.gov
Provides free access to MEDLINE, AIDSLINE, AIDSDRUGS, AIDSTRIALS, BIOETHICSLINE, ChemID, DIRLINE, HealthSTAR, HISTLINE, HSRPROJ, OLDMEDLINE, POPLINE, SDILINE, SPACELINE, and TOXLINE. Offers full range of Medical Subject Heading (MeSH) search features via UMLS Metathesaurus.

Martindale's Health Science Guide
www-sci.lib.uci.edu/HSG/HSGuide.html
Contact: Jim Martindale, jimmartindale@hotbot.com
A "Multimedia Specialized Information Resource" currently containing over 55,500 teaching files; over 126,300 medical cases; 1,055 multimedia courses/textbooks; 1,450 multimedia tutorials; over 3,430 databases, and over 10,400 movies.

Medicine Net
www.medicinenet.com
A network of doctors producing comprehensive, up-to-date health information for the public. Diseases, news, treatments, medical dictionary, first aid, and health facts.

Medical Matrix
www.medmatrix.org/
Contact: matrixeditors@slackinc.com
Must be registered to use the matrix, but no fees to use or register. Search the database by specialties, disease, clinical practice, literature, education, and more.

Mednets
www.internets.com/mednets/index.html
Contact: pgregor@mednets.com
Largest organized medical databases . . . the latest news in health care, the Websites of all the best online medical journals, medical schools' search engines. You will also find international specialty and regional associations in medicine, nursing, physiotherapy, and dentistry.

Medicine on the Net
www.mednet-i.com/aboutmedonthene2686.cfm
It is subscription only full-text access.

Medweb Plus
www.medwebplus.com/
Contact: http://medwebplus.com/comments.html
Searchable biomedical directory that catalogs both online and print information sources.

Mental Health Net Professional Resources
www.cmhc.com/prof.htm
Contact: webmaster@cmhc.com
This metasite contains databases for both the professional and the consumer covering all areas of mental health such as disorders, treatments, services, and publications.

Medscape
www.medscape.com/
Contact: editor@mail.medscape.com
Site for physicians with information regarding clinical management, practice guidelines, journal summaries and full-text articles, CME, and physicians discussions.

Multimedia Medical Reference Library
www.med-library.com/medlibrary/
This site is among the Net's premiere sources for reviewed medical information. All links within this "virtual" medical library have been carefully selected to represent the best and most current information in their respective fields.

National Institutes of Health (NIH)
www.nih.gov
Contact: NIHInfo@OD.NIH.GOV
Huge Website with links to all 25 of the National Institutes of Health, which are databases of their specific health information and resources. NIH also has information on health resources (subject-word guide), NIH publications, funding, and scientific news.

Nutritional Navigator
http://navigator.tufts.edu/
Contact: navigator@tufts.edu

A rating guide to nutrition Websites. Tufts University evaluates and rates quarterly the Websites that relate to nutrition.

OMNI
http://omni.ac.uk/
Contact: Bob Parkinson, Technical Officer; bob.parkinson@omni.ac.uk
Primarily a gateway to Internet resources in medicine, biomedicine, allied health, health management, and related topics.

OncoLink
http://oncolink.upenn.edu
Contact: editors@oncolink.upenn.edu
Comprehensive information about specific types of cancer, updates on cancer treatments, and news about research advances.

ONHealth.com
(http://onhealth.com/)

P. F. Anderson - Professional Links
www-personal.umich.edu/~pfa/pro/prolinks.html
Contact: P. F. "Pat" Anderson, pfa@umich.edu
This Web page provides links to many of author's favorite medical (as well as technical-type) databases and search engines; no annotations.

PEDINFO
www.pedinfo.org
Contact: S. Andrew (Andy) Spooner, aspooner@peds.uab.edu
These searchable databases are specific to pediatric health and medicine.

U.S. Food and Drug Administration
www.fda.gov/
Contact: www.fda.gov/comments.html
These directories not only inform about drugs and food, but also cosmetics, tobacco, medical devices, and products, toxicology. Other sections have specific information for patients, consumers, health professionals, state and local officials, even kids.

WebMD
(www.webmd.com)

See **Collection Development Related Discussion Groups, E-serials and Guides, Evaluation Guides, and Workshops** Webliography in Chapter One for discussion lists, newsgroups, e-serials, and other resources cited in this chapter.

5
Collecting Web-based Legal Information Resources

> "The information contained in this Website, and its associated Websites, including but not limited to FindLaw, the CyberSpace Law Center, the LawCrawler, LegalMinds, and the University Law Review Project, is provided as a service to the Internet community, and does not constitute legal advice. We try to provide quality information, but we make no claims, promises, or guarantees about the accuracy, completeness, or adequacy of the information contained in or linked to this Website and its associated sites. As legal advice must be tailored to the specific circumstances of each case, and laws are constantly changing, nothing provided herein should be used as a substitute for the advice of competent counsel."
> **FindLaw Disclaimer www.findlaw.com/info/disclaimer.html**

Legal Internet Resource Collection and Evaluation

The FindLaw (www.findlaw.com) Website disclaimer which introduces this chapter serves two purposes. First it establishes the conditions under which the FindLaw metasite provides its legal resources e-library. Second it exemplifies the conditions under which most Internet legal information is supplied.

Legal information is very sensitive. Incorrect legal information can lead to library clients losing money, their families, their homes, or even going to prison. It is, therefore, imperative that e-library collectors make a special effort in evaluating Internet legal information. Librarians and library staff should never under any circumstances offer legal advice. We can answer a client's questions but we cannot solve their problems. The possible exception to this rule is law librarians that hold the J.D. or other law degree who may elect to act as a lawyer. It is important to refer clients to legal counsel when the answers to their questions are beyond the scope of merely providing legal information.

Legal research impacts on just about every other field. For example, patents searching and trademark and copyright information are included in the Core Internet Legal Ready-Reference Collection in Chapter Two because they all involve the legal identification of intellectual property ownership. However, patent, trademark, and copyright information is also frequently associated with business, sciences and technology research as well.

Most legal resources are supplied by governmental agencies, legal organizations, law schools, or law firms. Some of the best primary resources—codes and court reports, for example—are those made freely available by the Government Printing Office through their GPO Access Website (www.access. gpo.gov/su_docs/) and the Cornell University Law School's Legal Information Institute Website (www.law.cornell.edu/). Much of the legal information to be found on the Internet is in raw form; full-text court reports, bills, court reports, and codes. Although it is free, it is not as searchable, nor does it have the many mechanisms for generating reports and analyzing data, as commercial products such as Lexis/Nexis and Westlaw have. In fact both of those fee-based services are Web-accessible. However, they are expensive. Lawyers, legal paraprofessionals, and law school students with access to the commercial services will find them much more efficient to use than the equivalent Internet sources. For the consumer and small business person, however, the Internet is good inexpensive access to basic information.

The Internet Legal Information Resource Collection Plan

What Purpose Will Your Web-based Legal Information E-library Collection Serve? For Whom are You Collecting Internet Legal Information Resources?

These collection-planning questions are strongly interrelated in any subject collection planning. In collecting legal resources they are virtually the same question. Will your collection be supporting research by legal professionals or consumers? Business professionals? Healthcare professionals? Students? Law school students? K–12 students?

Who your clients are defines the kinds of legal information you will include in your e-library. Some legal resources available through the Internet contain information that is highly complex and intended for legal professionals. Other sites focus on legal information in particular professional areas such as business, healthcare, science and technology, and so on. Some information on the Internet is written for the consumer. Even more information is intended for law school students. Legal information intended for children of various ages is difficult to find, although not impossible. For example, the United States Office of the President provides the "White House for Kids" Website with legal and political information intended for young people (www.whitehouse. gov/).

What Internet Legal Information Resources Will You Link to Through Your E-library?

Internet legal information resources take the following forms that can be described in terms of traditional reference source types. An annotated Legal Core Internet Ready-Reference Collection at the end of this section lists essential Internet reference tools organized by these reference source types:

1. Directories of lawyers, law schools, legal services, etc.
2. Dictionaries of legal terms (although there are no exceptional legal dictionaries posted on the Internet).
3. Abstracts, indexes, and table of contents services for legal serials—UnCover provides table of contents information for many law journals such as the *ABA Journal* and the *Computer and Telecommunications Law Review*.
4. Encyclopedias of legal information.
5. Legal e-serials.
6. Bibliographies of legal information sources (see the Webliographies of Legal Metasites at the end of this chapter).
7. Legal news.
8. Key primary documents including the state and federal codes, court reports, current legislation, and more.

The most valuable legal information on the Internet is in the form of full-text searchable databases containing U.S., international, state, and specialized legal codes, court decisions at all levels, as well as full-text access to U.S. bill tracking. In recent months, many premier law journals have been publishing full-text on the Internet. Most of these can be located by using the FindLaw metasite (www.findlaw.com).

How Will You Organize Your Internet Legal Information Resources?

In terms of legal information provided for consumers, an organizational structure which stresses the kind of questions that the resource assists in answering might be useful. For example, a collection of materials which provide information on divorce, bankruptcy, lemon laws, property laws, liability laws, adoption, landlord-tenant laws, and other legal problems that people commonly cope with.

Legal professionals or law school students might find an organization by jurisdiction and type of code most accessible.

Identifying and Collecting Internet Legal Information Resources

Websites Which Review and Evaluate Internet Legal Information Resources: Other E-libraries, Subject Collection Guides/Webliographies, Etc.

In terms of annotations, evaluations, and scope of subject coverage, the Internet Legal Resource Guide (www.ilrg.com/) is exemplary. The 'Lectric Law Library (www.lectlaw.com/) is also a very useful site for identifying and collecting quality legal Internet resources. There are several other excellent metasites listed in the Webliography for this chapter.

Discussion Lists and Newsgroups Where Individual Participants Review and Evaluate Internet Legal Information Resources

Cornell Law Library provides a service called the "Big Ear" (http://barratry.law.cornell.edu:5123/notify/buzz.html), which

> . . . listens to a variety of law-related mailing lists and newsgroups. From each, it selects messages which contain references to Net documents, and constructs a convenient cumulative listing which shows the title of the document, a link to it, and a link to the message "announcing" it on the mailing list. At the end of a week's time, the old listing is scrapped and a new one started. It thus offers a (slightly distorted) view of what's new on the Net for lawyers, and of what people are talking about.
>
> At the moment, BigEar listens to:
> **LAWSRC-L**, including postings from the Virtual Law Library submissions robot;
> **NET-LAWYERS;**
> **TEKNOIDS;**
> **LAW-LIB;**
> **LEGAL-WEBMASTERS;** and
> **INT-LAW.**

The discussion list LAWSRC-L is devoted entirely to reviewing and discussing Internet legal resources. The core discussion lists for law librarians are Law-lib and Lawlibref-L. Both of these discussion lists encourage discussion of Internet legal information resources as well as many other topics of interest to law librarians. Use the Web Law Lists and Discussion Groups site at www.washlaw.edu/listserv.html to find additional legal discussion lists and newsgroups.

E-journals and E-newsletters Which Publish Reviews and Evaluations of Internet Legal Information Resources

InSITE is an e-serial which reviews and annotates Internet legal information Websites. It is published by the Cornell Law Library (www.lawschool. cornell.edu/lawlibrary/insite.html*). The Law Library Resource Exchange* (www.llrx.com) is an outstanding current awareness "Webzine" which not only publishes legal Website reviews but also publishes articles discussing all aspects of legal information on the Internet. There are dozens of other e-journals and e-newsletters with Internet resource reviews published by law schools, law organizations, and commercial information providers. The best way to locate them is by searching the NewJour archives (http://gort.ucsd.edu/newjour/) or the *ARL Directory of Electronic Journals, Newsletters, and Academic Discussion Lists* companion database Website (www.arl.org).

Print Books and Journals Which Review Internet Resources

Of the several current Internet legal research books, *Law, Law, Law on the Internet: The Best Legal Websites and More* (1998*)* stands out as a resource for selecting Internet legal information resources. In co-author Rick Klau's words:

> *Law Law Law* is our attempt to sort out the good from the bad. Other books set out to list *every* legal Website, while others list a handful—and we felt that neither approach was sufficient. A directory leads you on too many wild goose chases, while a handful makes you wonder if the author really looked at everything out there. The result is *Law Law Law on the Internet*: a combination of editorial comments about what works and what doesn't in the legal market, and a list of the best examples of Websites that are useful for lawyers and legal researchers. (from the Amazon.com review of the book)

Four other current books are listed in the "Print and Electronic Publications Cited or Consulted in this Chapter" section at the end of this chapter. They are primarily general legal research guides with discussions or tutorials on Internet legal research. All of them include annotated links to Internet legal information resources.

Most law journals which publish book reviews are now including Internet resource reviews. Three in particular were identified as useful by Lawlibref-L subscribers: *Law Practice Management, The Internet Lawyer,* and *Legal Assistant Today.* Library-oriented serials including *Choice, Library Journal, College and Research Libraries,* and *American Libraries*, also review Internet legal information Websites.

Evaluating Internet Legal Information Resources

Legal information has, as does business and medical information, the power to affect library clients' financial and physical well-being. Bad legal information might mean a library client will go to prison or lose their home or children. Although library staff cannot under any circumstances provide legal advice to library clients, they must know enough about legal information to evaluate legal information resources. Use the strategies described in Chapter One to find the answers to the following questions about Internet legal information resources.

Who Provided the Information? What is Their Reputation as an Information Provider? Does the Information Provider Have the Authority or Expertise to Provide Information on That Topic?

This information must be crystal clear. If it is even a bit difficult to locate on a legal information Website then the information is suspect. For example, look at the Website for *Black's Law Dictionary* (www.alaska.net/~winter/ black_law_dictionary.html). Then look at the printed version of *Black's Law Dictionary*, search for it in your library OPAC, or locate the publication information on Amazon.com (www.amazon.com). What is the first thing you notice about the *Black's Law Dictionary* site? There is no attribution on the page, nor any links to an attribution information page. However, the "real" *Black's Law Dictionary* and both the OPAC and Amazon.com records reveal the authors and publishers of the *Black's Law Dictionary*. Now look at the URL in the address/location box in your Web browser. Back space over the "black_law_dictionary.html" part, so that the URL is www.alaska.net/~winter and press <return>. This will show you the information provider for the information resource called "Black's Law Dictionary" which is on the Web at www.alaska.net/~winter/black_law_dictionary.html. This individual is not the actual author nor is his organization the actual publisher of the *Black's Law Dictionary*.

Is the Information Provided for Current Information or for Historical Purposes? Does Currency or Lack of Currency Affect the Quality of the Information? When was the Last Update of the Information?

All legal information is time sensitive. Laws expire, are amended, are passed, are found unconstitutional, are reinterpreted by courts, and become obsolete. It is important that Internet legal information resources clearly state the version of legal codes and the dates of court decisions.

Is Security Important in Interacting with a Given Internet Information Source? Is a Site Likely to be Hacked and Information Altered? Will Personal or Financial Information be Requested From Clients?

Security of legal information Websites is very important. It is unlikely that a legal information Website will request financial or personal information from clients. If there is any doubt about security, then contact the Website owner and ask.

Is Privacy of Information-Seeking Behavior an Important Factor for You or Your Clients?

Privacy is an issue for clients looking for personal legal information such as divorce or bankruptcy laws.

Selecting a Core Internet Legal Ready-reference Collection

Selection criteria for any kind of legal information resources are derived from the answers arrived at during the collection-planning process. You may also use an existing legal ready-reference collection as a model to compare the Internet ready-reference tools against. Figure 5.1 lists the core legal ready-reference tools that subscribers to Publib and Libref-L said they could not live without. The access, design, and content criteria for assessing the value of Websites for library users are reproduced in Table 5.1. The Legal Internet ready-reference core collection included below was compiled with these criteria in mind. The intended client groups are English-speaking adults who are looking for basic legal information for personal, educational or professional purposes. All of these Websites adhere to international Web browser standards. Most of them provide legal information such as codes, law reviews, court reports and other primary documents at no cost to the consumer. Several also offer special fee-based services. Archiving of these legal information Websites is usually in print or magnetic tape format. Most of the free primary information is also available in value-added commercial databases such as Lexis/Nexis and Westlaw.

**Figure 5.1   June 15, 1999 Report on Core Legal Reference Tools
Posted to Libref-L and Publib**

Date: Tue, 15 Jun 1999 13:10:35 -0400
Subject: Survey Results: Core Reference Tools

===== Original Message From "Diane K. Kovacs" <diane@kovacs.com> =====

Thank you all very much to everyone who responded. Here are the core reference tools survey results from my previous question to this list (sorry for cross-posting inconveniences). They are in approximately order of their mention with some notes from me and comments from respondents. Please feel free to send me your core reference tools. I can always add to these. Thank you all again!

6. What are your two most used reference tools for law questions?

The number one source by a lot:
Specific state codes, regulations, and case reporters.

Others:
West's Encyclopedia of American Law
Nolo Press books on divorce, bankruptcy, copyright, trademark, and patents
Black's Law Dictionary
GPO Access - through internet
Thomas online - through internet
WESTLAW CD-ROM (Massachusetts Laws, Regs, Cases)
Martindale-Hubbel
Tenant/Landlord Law (various sources - mostly local)
Legal Forms publications
BOCA codes (Building Officials and Code Administrators) for regulations on various building projects
Divorce in Ohio

Other areas added:
"Two areas I didn't have room for are Native Americans (Encyclopedia of Native American Tribes by Waldman) and information about what happened in different eras (Time-Life series of the Gale Decades series)"

Table 5.1 Content Criteria for Internet Resources

Selection Adapted from Caywood (1996) (http://www6.pilot.infi.net/~carolyn/criteria.html)

1. Does the resource meet some current awareness related information need of the e-library's intended clients?
2. Does the resource provide the information at a level and language suitable to the age, educational background, and subject interests of the e-library's intended clients?
3. Does the resource provide information in a form that you want to include in your e-library? News services or e-serials, for example.

Other Selection Criteria Specific to Internet Resources Are:

4. Access and Design
   Will the e-library's intended clients have the computer equipment and software needed to use the resource? Does the resource allow for access by disabled individuals who may need to use text-to-voice software or other enabling tool? Does the resource display in the Web browser within a reasonable amount of time?

5. Archiving
   Will the information provider provide "back issues" or archives of the resource? Will you need to make arrangements to store such information locally if needed? This is especially important in the case of e-serials or current information that will become valuable historical information over time. Most social sciences research information will require some kind of archiving arrangements be made. It doesn't really matter if the information is archived in print publications, backed up to CD-ROM, magnetic tape or other electronic storage media, or simply kept available on the Web for an indeterminate period as long as researchers are assured that it will be archived and available in the future.

6. Cost/Licensing/User Access Control
   Some Internet accessible resources are fee-based. If that is the case, for example as with the *Encyclopedia Britannica* online, consideration will need to be made for not only the cost of the resource, but any licensing arrangements or user access control that must be exercised. For example, will the resource only be accessible by users from within the library's domain or can any library user from any location by using a login and password or library card number access the resource.

Legal Core Internet Ready-reference Collection

Directories
West Legal Directory
www.lawoffice.com/ Lawyer Location service, "The Informed Client" legal information collection, as well as "Attorney Resources."

Martindale-Hubbell
www.martindale.com/
Lawyer locator & misc. sites collection.

Dictionaries
OneLook Dictionaries, The Faster Finder
www.onelook.com/
The ultimate Internet dictionary lookup site. Search 475 general and specialized English dictionaries simultaneously, or select the ones you want to search. More than two million words now indexed.—[Annotation from LII]

Bibliographies—See *Webliography of Legal Metasites*

Abstracts and Indexes
KeyCite
www.keycite.com/
Citation law research service. Fee to use this site.

Table of Contents Services
UnCover
http://uncweb.carl.org/
Contents information of 18,000 journal titles. There is free access to the UnCover database to look at citations. Faxed, e-mail, or postal document delivery is fee-based.

Encyclopedias
Nolo's Legal Encyclopedia
www.nolo.com/briefs.html
Consumer oriented legal information in 15 different categories of common sense language legal information. Includes information on family law, patents and copyright, as well as small-business related legal information.

News (Current Events)
CNN
http://cnn.com

Full-text version of the CNN news reports and features. Updated continuously. Archives searchable.

Court TV Online
www.courttv.com/
Full-text reports and archives on legal events covered by Court TV.

Key Primary Documents (annual reports, law codes, statistical, and sources)
Copyright Office of the U.S. Library of Congress
http://lcweb.loc.gov/copyright/

GPO Access on the Web Full-text
www.access.gpo.gov
Searchable access to the Federal Register, Code of Federal Regulations, Congressional Documents, Directory and Index, The Budget of the U.S. Government, and more. Made available through the GPO Website (has the Code of Federal Regulations) or Purdue University Libraries.

Legal Information Institute - Cornell Law School
www.law.cornell.edu/
Full-text searchable U.S. Revised Code, Constitution of the United States, and a collection of law codes by state and jurisdiction and a fine international law collection.

U.S. Patent and Trademark Office Patent Databases
http://patents.uspto.gov/
As of March 1999 the U.S. Patent and Trademark Office Patent Databases include free full-text and image access to patents from 1976 to present. The search and retrieval functions are simple and do not allow complex reports to be generated.

U.S. Patent and Trademark Office
www.uspto.gov/
Free, full-text, and image searchable database of registered trademarks.

White House for Kids
www.whitehouse.gov/

• •

E-library Builder Story

Michigan Electronic Library (MEL)

The Library of Michigan and the University of Michigan, University Libraries
http://mel.lib.mi.us
Contact: Sue Davidsen davidsen@umich.edu

Way back in 1992, in the middle of the night, Sue Davidsen, director of the Michigan Electronic Library (MEL), woke up thinking about creating an e-library of Internet resources organized by subject using Gopher.

> . . . when the University of Michigan's GoMLink program was supporting the state's public libraries with reference service, my manager and I were trying to find a way to make the Internet easier for our public librarians and we had invested in a UNIX machine and Gopher software. Rather than organize information a la the U of Minnesota's view, I woke up thinking, "why don't we organize it by subject?" We were the first to do that, making us the first virtual library on the Internet. Back then I was a reference librarian for MLink and the Gopher was called GoMLink.

In 1995, the Library of Michigan offered GoMLink federal Library Services and Technology Act (LSTA) funds from the Department of Education to convert to a Web version. At the same time, GoMLink began to include electronic resources other than Internet resources. The name was changed to Michigan Electronic Library, or MEL.

Davidsen explains the further evolution of MEL:

> As time has gone on, MEL has become the user interface for all of Michigan's research info projects. For example, we now have commercial databases Firstsearch, IAC Reference Gold, and IAC Health Web available to Michigan residents (this piece of MEL is the idea of George Needham, our state librarian who applied to and received funds from the state legislature for this). We also have a statewide serial database called SPAN, a GPO Access gateway, and the Michigan Legislature's bills, calendars, laws, etc. MEL is very broadly supported and contributed to in the state. Michigan State University provides periodical article delivery for the commercial databases when the full text is not available. MEL's Internet gateway piece as well as administration for the user interface is hosted here at the University of Michigan Library. The legislature's site and SPAN are coming

from the Library of Michigan. This is truly a statewide, multi-type library project.

The University of Michigan Library administration approved of the GoMLink program. Davidsen's boss, Dick Hathaway, was the coordinator of the GoMLink program. The original project, funded by the Kellogg Foundation, was initiated to provide ways to make the Internet more accessible to the state's public librarians. No formal collection plan was written, but the GoMLink program was developed in line with the original project goals. MEL was a Web-based continuation of the original project.

The University of Michigan Library had no hardware or software in place to support the GoMLink project. Approximately $6,500 was spent to acquire a NeXt workstation, which ran UNIX. Later in 1995, the project purchased a Sun SPARCstation 20/50 and began running the Apache Web server software. The original Gopher software and the Apache Web server software were free.

Davidsen estimates that half her working time was spent creating the initial Gopher e-library. She is now the full-time director of MEL. For the original GoMLink Gopher e-library, she hired a programmer and learned UNIX system administration so she could maintain the Gopher. Subject experts were recruited to spend approximately ten hours per week evaluating and adding Internet sites.

> We had an initial face-to-face meeting to set our evaluation and collection guidelines, but then scattered, since we all live throughout the Midwest (and at one time throughout the country). Any new selectors are sent policies, etc., via e-mail and the training is very informal. As we have added the commercial databases, however, all of our selectors will be sent to formal training for all of those (formal training is provided by the Michigan Library Consortium).

These subject specialists are listed and identified at http://mel.lib.mi.us/about/melspecialists.html. The MEL Director, the subject specialists, and the staff at the Michigan Library Consortium who manage the commercial databases and training spend an estimated 220 hours per week. There are also members of the advisory group who give four hours per quarter and more.

MEL will continue to add commercial databases as directed by the state of Michigan. They also plan to undertake a retrospective conversion project to convert HTML links into a database that will conform to Dublin Core Metadata. The technology infrastructure will be upgraded and a commercial search engine will be bought and installed to improve the search capability.

For Michigan weather
follow the sun!

The Michigan Electronic Library

 Magazines and Periodicals [commercial databases available to Michigan residents only]

Browse the
Internet by
Subject:

- Business, Economics & Labor
- Children & Young Adults
- Education
- Government, Politics & Law
- Health Information Resources
- Humanities & the Arts
- The Internet & Computers

- Libraries & Information Science
- Michigan
- News, Media & Periodicals
- Recreation & Leisure
- Reference Desk
- Science & the Environment
- Social Issues & Social Services

Search MEL

About MEL

Michigan Libraries

**Span: A list of magazines
held in Michigan libraries**

Michigan Government Information

Michigan Communities

Director of the Michigan Electronic Library: Sue Davidsen (davidsen@mel.org)

This project is sponsored by the Library of Michigan and the University of Michigan, University Library.
It is funded, in part, with Library Services & Technology Act (LSTA) funds
administered by the Library of Michigan. The MEL server is hosted by Merit Network.

 Funded in part through the Institute of Museum and Library Services

webmaster@mel.org

Michigan Electronic Library (MEL)

Print and Electronic Publications Cited or Consulted in Chapter Five

"Big Ear." Cornell Law Library. (http://barratry.law.cornell.edu:5123/notify/buzz.html).

Elias, S. R., Levinkind, S., and Portman J. 1998. *Legal Research Online and in the Library.* Berkeley: Nolo Press.

Find Law. "FindLaw Disclaimer." (www.findlaw.com/info/disclaimer.html).

Heels, E.J. and Klau, R.P. 1998. *Law, Law, Law on the Internet: The Best Legal Websites and More.* Chicago: American Bar Association.

Lawson J. 1999. *The Complete Internet Handbook for Lawyers.* American Bar Association, Law Practice Management Section.

Law Quickly & Easily on the Internet. NetGuide Publishing.

Pollin S. 1999. *Law Quickly & Easily on the Internet.* NetGuide Publishing.

Review of *Law, Law, Law on the Internet: The Best Legal Websites and More.* Amazon.com (www.Amazon.com)

Webliographies Included with Chapter Five

Legal Resource Metasites

"Big Ear"—Cornell Law Library
http://barratry.law.cornell.edu:5123/notify/buzz.html

Findlaw
http://findlaw.com
Contact: write@findlaw.com
Comprehensive site of foreign, U.S., and state laws, legal services, references, and information.

HITS - HyperText Index Tracking Systems (U.S. patent pending)
www.hyperindex.com/
Contact: Steve Kelfer, cars@stic.net.
Legal information service sponsored by the Texas Center for Public Information in order to demonstrate that public information can be provided at low cost regardless of volume through the Internet. Access to thousands of documents including U.S. legal opinions and decisions, not just Texas.

Internet Law Library
http://law.house.gov/
and/or
http://uscode.house.gov
Contact: usc@mail.house.gov
Site of U.S. and foreign law, law schools, lawyer directory, and other legal sources.

Internet Legal Resource Guide
www.ilrg.com/
A categorized index of more than 4,000 select Websites in 238 nations, islands, and territories, as well as more than 850 locally-stored Web pages and downloadable files. This site was established to serve as a comprehensive resource of the information available on the Internet concerning law and the legal profession, with an emphasis on the United States of America. Designed for everyone, lay persons and legal scholars alike, it is quality controlled to include only the most substantive legal resources online. The selection criteria are predicated on two principles: the extent to which the resource is unique, as well as the relative value of the information it provides.

LawGuru.com
www.lawguru.com/
Metasite which includes multi-site legal information search tools as well as annnoted links to legal Websites.

Law Library Resource Exchange
www.llrx.com
Contact: Sabrina I. Pacifici or Cindy L. Chick, editors@llrx.com.
A Webzine with special focus on research, management, and technology topics for legal professionals.

'Lectric Law Library
www.lectlaw.com/
Comprehensive annotated site. Difficult site design outweighed by quality and quantity of resources included.

WashLaw Web
www.washlaw.edu
Contact: Mark Folmsbee; zzfolm@washburn.edu
Web links relating types, areas, and states laws.

Web Law Lists and Discussion Groups
http://lawlib.wuacc.edu/washlaw/listserv.html
Contact: Joe Hewitt, zzhewitt@washburn.edu
This service from the Washburn University School of Law can be used for a legal resource and research aid.

See **Collection Development Related Discussion Groups, E-serials and Guides, Evaluation Guides, and Workshops** Webliography in Chapter Two for discussion lists, newsgroups, e-serials and other resources cited in this chapter.

6
Collecting Web-based Biological Science, Social and Physical Sciences, and Technology Information Resources

> "In assessing the impact of the Internet on science and technology, it is important to bear in mind that scientists engaged in global networking long before the Internet. Research success has always depended on close communication and resource sharing with colleagues around the world. Scientists have always been skilled in retrieving data from distributed sources worldwide and synthesizing them into a logical whole. And, for hundreds of years, scientists have been communicating their ideas and knowledge in the form of a scientific paper, proposal, or presentation—to a forum of peers for comment, critical review, questioning, and judgement.
>
> Before the emergence of worldwide computer internetworks, scientists accomplished these tasks by applying the technologies of the day: postal delivery, phone, fax, printed media such as the science journal, and transportation to join colleagues in the lab, field, or conference. Now they use electronic mail, discussion groups, File Transfer Protocol, Telnet, Gopher, and the World Wide Web to accomplish the same. . . . the Internet has enabled scientists to perform ordinary tasks more efficiently, quickly, and effectively."
>
> Clements, G. 1996, *Science and Technology on the Internet*.
> Berkeley, CA: Library Solutions Press. p. xvii.

Biological Science, Social and Physical Sciences, and Technology Internet Resource Collection and Evaluation

Collecting, evaluating, and selecting scientific information resources is a relatively complex process. Much scientific information requires resource collectors to either have some subject expertise or to have access to someone else who has subject expertise. The collection of Internet biological, social and physical science, and technology resources will be discussed in this chapter. The need for non-subject specialists to consult with subject specialists in the process of collecting, evaluating, and selecting scientific information resources from the Internet is emphasized.

Biological science resources include biomedical research sources as well as botany, zoology, environmental science, and resources in other biological science fields. The scope of biological science resources on the Internet is as broad and diverse as the biosphere of the earth. Biological science information resources on the Internet include: general introductions to biological concepts, complete full-text databases in specialized biological research areas, peer-reviewed biological science e-serials, and other specialized information archives in every biological sciences research area conceivable.

Social sciences subjects include anthropology, archaeology, economics, sociology, psychology, philosophy, and any other area related to the study of human cultures, societies, ideas, and minds. Most quality social sciences related Websites on the Internet are published by academic organizations. There are literally thousands of such Websites. Physical sciences and technology are often grouped together for collection purposes. The physical sciences include fields such as chemistry, physics, geology, and mathematics. Technology generally includes engineering and computer science.

Resources that support scientific study and education in the physical science and technologies were some of the first to appear on the Internet. Specifically, computer science information was the first technical information distributed through the Internet.

The Internet Science and Technology Information Resource Collection Plan

What Purposes Will Your Web-based Science and Technology E-library Collection Serve? What Subjects Will be Included and for Whom are You Collecting Internet Resources?

Biological science information will probably be used primarily by students and researchers. The important aspects to be aware of are age and educational level of the clients. School librarians, as with other categories of scientific information, will probably want to collect biological sciences information resources designed for k–12 students. Public librarians will need to serve not only the k–12 students, but other members of the public who may want more or less complex information. Academic libraries will frequently be collecting for undergraduate, graduate, post-doctoral students, and biological science educators and researchers. Introductory biology resources might be needed in a k–12 library.

Social sciences information resources will nearly always be needed for use in an educational or research context. The important questions for selecting social science Internet resources are which subjects will be included in the collection and for what age group and educational level is the collection targeted. A social sciences information collection for a school or public library is likely to be designed for k–12 students to use in support of their education, as well as for other members of the community to use in an educational, professional, or business context. Academic libraries may need to collect resources both for college students and for the social scientists teaching and researching in their parent college or university. Special libraries may collect social sciences information that supports business or technology research in some way. Demographic data, marketing surveys, product testing, industrial design, and other social scientific information may be included.

As with the other types of scientific information discussed above, users of physical scientific information will most likely be students, of various ages and educational attainment, and researchers. Technology information may be needed by consumers or by professionals (such as engineers or computing professionals).

Special libraries serving physical science and technology researchers will need to acquire resources that provide depth of coverage in a specific area of scientific or technological information. For example, they may need to collect resources for geology, nuclear physics, manufacturing engineering, chemical synthesis, environmental engineering, computer engineering, and so on. Academic libraries may need to cover a broad range of physical science and technology topics, and also to cover them in-depth for researchers working in their parent institutions.

Each library should be aware of which scientific subject areas they support for researchers and students in their parent organizations.

What Internet Science and Technology Information Resources Will You Link to Through Your E-library?

Robert McGeachin's 1998 article "Selection Criteria for Web-Based Resources in a Science and Technology Library Collection," focuses on collection development for science and technology resources. He identifies:

> Internet-based materials that fit the needs of users of science and technology libraries include electronic journals and magazines, books and reference books, statistical sources and databases. (p. 2).

Internet biological science information resources take forms that can be described in terms of traditional reference source types. An annotated Biological, Social and Physical Sciences, and Technology Core Internet Ready-Reference Collection at the end of this section lists selected Internet reference tools organized by these reference source types:

1. Directories of scientists, science organizations, and projects.
2. Dictionaries of scientific terminology.
3. Abstracts, indexes, and table of contents services for scientific serials.
4. Encyclopedias of scientific information.
5. Sciences e-serials and databases.
6. Bibliographies of scientific information sources (see Webliographies of Science and Technology Metasites at the end of this chapter).
7. Science news services.
8. Key primary documents such as scientific research data.

How Will You Organize Your Internet Science and Technology Resources?

Internet science and technology resources can be organized by main subject and then by sub-fields and specialties. Some thought might be given to organizing the resources by level of education as well as by subject area.

Identifying and Collecting Internet Science and Technology Information Resources

Websites Which Review and Evaluate Internet Science and Technology Resources: Other E-libraries, Subject Collection Guides/Webliographies, Etc.

Several science and technology subject collections, metasites, and e-libraries are included in this chapter's Webliography. Most of them deal with a narrow range of physical science specialization such as the Sheffield ChemDex site (www.chemdex.org/) or the EELS—Engineering Electronic Library Sweden (eels.lub.lu.se/). One site, SciCentral (http://scicentral.com) does try to cover all areas of science in a metadatabase.

The INFOMINE–Comprehensive Biological, Agricultural, & Medical Internet Resource Collection (http://lib-www.ucr.edu/bioag/) and Anne Marie Malley's Biomedical and Life Sciences Sites (www.calacademy.org/research/library/biodiv/biblio/sla98.htm) are good sources of reviewed and annotated Websites for Internet biological sciences information resources.

The INFOMINE–Social Sciences and Humanities area at http://lib-www.ucr.edu/sshinfo.html, and the Argus Clearinghouse–Social Science and Social Issues section, at www.clearinghouse.net/cgi-bin/chadmin/viewcat/Social_Sciences___Social_Issues?kywd++, are good sources of reviewed and annotated lists of Internet social sciences information resources. The latter site lists several annotated collections of social sciences resources.

Discussion Lists and Newsgroups Where Individual Participants Review and Evaluate Internet Science and Technology Information Resources

Most of core discussion lists and newsgroups for the biological sciences Internet resources are part of the BIOSCI–Electronic Newsgroup Network for Biology (www.bio.net).

There is no global social science Internet resource discussion list or newsgroups. There are some groups which discuss social science Internet resources by specific topic. For example, ASIA-WWW-MONITOR discusses Websites for social science studies in and about Asia. Use The COOMBSWeb Social Sciences server at http://coombs.anu.edu.au/CoombsHome.html can help to find some specific social-science-related discussion lists.

The core discussion lists and newsgroups for physical science and technology Internet resources in libraries are STS-L, discussion of science and technology librarianship; SLA-Dite, discussion for the Information Technology Division of the Special Libraries Association; and ELDNET, discussion of the Engineering Libraries Division of the American Society of Engineering Education. All three sites include discussions and reviews of physical sciences and technology related Websites.

Other field-specific science and technology discussion lists can be searched in *The Directory of Scholarly and Professional Electronic Conferences* (www.arl.org/scomm/edir/) and The PHOAKS project (www.phoaks.com). Also, MATHQA is a discussion list which includes reviews of mathematical Websites.

E-journals and E-newsletters Which Publish Reviews and Evaluations of Internet Science and Technology Information Resources

The Internet Scout Project (http://scout.cs.wisc.edu/) serves science and engineering researchers and educators with the bi-weekly e-newsletter *The Scout Report for Science and Engineering* (SRSCIENG). *The Scout Report for Science and Engineering* publishes reviews of Internet biological and physical sciences information resources. The Finger Searcher Science Seeker Newsletter (www.connect.ab.ca/~xdr/fsearch/fsindex.html) publishes reviews of science resources on the Internet which are of interest to k–12 teachers and students, as well as some higher-education-related sites. The outstanding review source for Internet social sciences information resources is another Internet Scout Project publication (http://scout.cs.wisc.edu/). *The Scout Report for Social Sciences* (SRSOCSCI) publishes bi-weekly and reviews Internet resources of interest to researchers and educators in the social sciences.

Other e-serials which review Internet resources for various fields of physical science and technology can be identified by searching the NewJour archives (http://gort.ucsd.edu/newjour/) or the *ARL Directory of Electronic Journals, Newsletters,* and *Academic Discussion Lists* companion database Website (www.arl.org/scomm/edir/).

Print Books and Journals Which Review Internet Sciences and Technology Information Resources

The Internet for Scientists and Engineers (1997–98) by B. Thomas provides handpicked sites for scientists and engineers in 22 major science and technology areas. Thomas has pre-screened, evaluated, and annotated each site for suitability to the subject area, stability of the resource URL, and authority of the information providing agency, organization, or individual.

There are a number of other books which annotate and review Internet science and technology information resources included in the works cited section of this chapter. At this writing, however, most of them are out of date. It is very difficult for print publications to keep up with the changes and additions frequently made to Internet resources.

Many scientific serials include reviews of Internet resources within the text of articles or in their review sections. One in particular, *Genetic Engineering News* has a feature called Web Spinning. The author, Kevin Ahern, Ph.D.—biochemistry and biophysics at Oregon State University—reviews biochemistry and biophysics Websites. He also posts those reviews at www.davincipress.com/webspinning.html. Another example of a mainstream biological science newsletter which includes Website reviews is *ASM News* (the news magazine of the American Society for Microbiology). The print newsletter called *Feminist Collections* (www.library.wisc.edu/libraries/WomensStudies/fcmain.htm) is a good example of a social science serial which publishes Internet resource reviews. It is published by the University of Wisconsin System Librarian's Office. Every issue has information about new Internet resources related to women's studies in the arts, the humanities, the social sciences, and the sciences.

Evaluating Internet Science and Technology Information Resources

The key criteria for evaluating science and technology information resources is to determine the source of the data, the research and statistical methodologies used in collecting the information, and the authority of the information provider. Scientific information is often difficult for the non-subject specialist to evaluate, especially information provided at the research or higher-education levels. Each scientific field (such as anthropology, economics, botany, zoology, environmental sciences, computer science, engineering, chemistry, physics, and so on) has its own particular vocabulary and accepted research methodologies. Physical sciences and technology, in particular, use mathematical and symbolic notations that are not easily interpreted by the non-subject specialist. It will be more difficult for the non-subject specialist to judge the information content without consulting a subject specialist. At the k–12 educational level, or with materials provided specifically for the non-specialist, it will be important to verify that the information provider has the authority to write on a particular topic. It will also be important to determine if the information provider has experience in teaching k–12 level scientific subjects. As with most subject areas, the evaluation strategies for Internet information resources described in Chapter One will work very well for evaluating Internet science and technology information resources.

Selecting a Core Internet Science and Technology Ready-reference Collection

The critical element in efficiently collecting science and technology information resources from the Internet is to focus on the subject interests of your client community. The selection of science and technology information resources is highly dependent on the exact science or technology field for which you are collecting information resources. There is no need to collect everything that is available, for example, on "Indigenous Australian Anthropology" sites if your community, school, or organization does not have a program in Australian or Pacific cultural studies to support. Social sciences resources are frequently used in business research. For example, demographics data, psychological profiling, market research, and economic trend information are all used in business. The criteria for assessing the value of Websites for library clients are reproduced in Table 6.1. The most important guidelines for selection are given in the list of access, design, and content criteria. This additional criteria is related to the first three standard selection criteria. Selection must be made in the subject fields and sub-specialties represented by the library's clients. Furthermore, selection must be made at the education or complexity level required by those clients. For example, high-energy physics research scientists studying the quark will need very different materials from the high school physics students studying relativity. The science and technology Internet ready-reference core collection included below was compiled with these criteria in mind. The intended client group is, very broadly, any English-speaking adult who might be interested in ready-reference scientific research information at a post-secondary school educational level. The access and design of all these core science and technology ready-reference Internet resources are based on standards of simplicity and international Internet Web browser compatibility with no special software required for access. Some of these sites do offer special instructional or graphics software for download. Most of them are free of direct cost with some having special fee-based services. Archiving of most of the critical information at these sites is assured by the researchers who provided the information.

Table 6.1 Content Criteria for Internet Resources

Selection Adapted from Caywood (1996) (http://www6.pilot.infi.net/~carolyn/criteria.html)

1. Does the resource meet some current awareness related information need of the e-library's intended clients?
2. Does the resource provide the information at a level and language suitable to the age, educational background, and subject interests of the e-library's intended clients?
3. Does the resource provide information in a form that you want to include in your e-library? News services or e-serials, for example.

Other Selection Criteria Specific to Internet Resources Are:

4. Access and Design
   Will the e-library's intended clients have the computer equipment and software needed to use the resource? Does the resource allow for access by disabled individuals who may need to use text-to-voice software or other enabling tool? Does the resource display in the Web browser within a reasonable amount of time?

5. Archiving
   Will the information provider provide "back issues" or archives of the resource? Will you need to make arrangements to store such information locally if needed? This is especially important in the case of e-serials or current information that will become valuable historical information over time. Most social sciences research information will require some kind of archiving arrangements be made. It doesn't really matter if the information is archived in print publications, backed up to CD-ROM, magnetic tape or other electronic storage media, or simply kept available on the Web for an indeterminate period as long as researchers are assured that it will be archived and available in the future.

6. Cost/Licensing/User Access Control
   Some Internet accessible resources are fee-based. If that is the case, for example as with the *Encyclopedia Britannica* online, consideration will need to be made for not only the cost of the resource, but any licensing arrangements or user access control that must be exercised. For example, will the resource only be accessible by users from within the library's domain or can any library user from any location by using a login and password or library card number access the resource.

Biological Science, Social and Physical Sciences, and Technology Core Internet Ready-reference Collection

BIOLOGICAL SCIENCES:
Directories
WWW Virtual Library: Biotechnology
www.cato.com/biotech/
Lists companies involved in pharmaceutical research, biotech products and services, educational opportunities for pharmaceutical and biotech training and degree programs, and online and print publications in the drug and biotech field.

Directories of Biologists
www.york.biosis.org/zrdocs/desktop/biol_dir.htm
Alphabet list of a hundred or so directories listing contact information for biologists.

Dictionaries
OneLook Dictionaries, The Faster Finder
www.onelook.com/
The ultimate Internet dictionary lookup site. Search 475 general and specialized English dictionaries simultaneously, or select the ones you want to search. More than two million words now indexed.—[Annotation from LII]

Life Sciences Dictionary
http://biotech.icmb.utexas.edu/search/dict-search.html
8300 plus terms deal with biochemistry, biotechnology, botany, cell biology, and genetics. This is not included in OneLook Dictionaries.

Bibliographies
See *Webliography of Science and Technology Metasites*

Abstracts and Indexes
PubMed
www.ncbi.nlm.nih.gov/PubMed/
NLM's search service to access the nine million citations in MEDLINE and Pre-MEDLINE (with links to participating online journals), and other related databases.

AGRICOLA
www.nal.usda.gov/ag98/ag98.html This free Web service for the essential agriculture database requires searching of book and journal citations separately. Journal citations date from 1979 to present.

Table of Contents Services
Elsevier Contents Direct
www.elsevier.nl/homepage/alert.htt?mode=direct
A free e-mail service which delivers Elsevier Science book and journal tables of contents directly to your PC, providing you with the very latest information on soon-to-be published research.

Elsevier Contents Search
www.elsevier.nl/homepage/alert.htt?mode=contents&main
Provides online tables of contents for more than 1100 Elsevier Science journals, and author index and keyword search facilities, plus journal volumes and issues listed per year.

UnCover
http://uncweb.carl.org/
Contents information of 18,000 journal titles. There is free access to the UnCover database to look at citations. Faxed, e-mail, or postal document delivery is fee-based.

Encyclopedias
The Animal Diversity Web
www.oit.itd.umich.edu/projects/ADW/
The Animal Diversity Web is a collection of pictures and information about animals. Accounts of individual species include information on distributions, natural history, conservation, and economic importance, along with pictures and sounds if available. Synopses of some higher taxonomic groups are also provided. The information is arranged in a taxonomic hierarchy for ease of navigation, and "shortcuts" (either through searching for specific names or characteristics or through direct links to some taxa) make it simple to find particular species or groups of species. . . . The majority of species accounts available on the Animal Diversity Web were written by students (including the gray wolf account). We review most accounts, but we can not guarantee their accuracy or completeness. [Annotation from ADW]

BioTech: Life Sciences Resources and Reference Tools
http://biotech.icmb.utexas.edu/
A hybrid biology/chemistry educational resource and research tool. Maintained by a project team of faculty from several universities.

Encyclopedia Smithsonian
www.si.edu/resource/faq/start.htm
The Smithsonian Institution receives a great many public inquiries covering a wide range of topics. Therefore, the following responses have been compiled to answer frequently asked questions or to provide guidance in finding the requested information. New information will be added continually. Life science topics covered include: agriculture, biodiversity, botany, bugs, chemistry, environmental science, horticulture, mammals, zoology, and more.

E-serials
Nature
www.nature.com/
Fee based for full-text access, but free registration allows you to: browse the tables of contents and first paragraphs, perform searches, and sign up for a free weekly summary of *Nature*'s table of contents by e-mail.

Scientific American
www.sciam.com/
Online counterpart to the well-known print magazine. Provides full-text and enhanced (hypertext) copies of selected articles that appeared in print, news, and reviews. Also includes a list of the editors' favorite bookmarks as well as an ask-the-experts section.

News (Current Events)
BioOnline
http://bio.com/
The News and Events department provides information from industry publishers and organizations on current events, meetings, conferences, and legislation. This site also has a directory of biotechnology companies, biotech products, and links to other biological journals and newsletters.

The Scientist
www.the-scientist.library.upenn.edu/
Edited by Eugene Garfield, there is free access to this online version of the magazine which calls itself "The News Journal for the Life Scientist." It includes news stories, links to working papers on the Web, job listings, and notices of meetings.

Key Primary Documents
   (annual reports, law codes, and statistical sources)
Code of Federal Regulations
www.access.gpo.gov/nara/cfr/cfr-table-search.html
Important for food regulations, endangered species, etc.

Chemicool
www-tech.mit.edu/Chemicool/
Interactive Period Table of Elements which provides information about each element.

NSF, Division of Science Resources Studies
www.nsf.gov/sbe/srs/stats.htm
Provides full-text access to statistical reports of the NSF as well as links to other important science statistics sites.

SOCIAL SCIENCES:
Dictionaries
OneLook Dictionaries, The Faster Finder
www.onelook.com/
The ultimate Internet dictionary lookup site. Search 475 general and specialized English dictionaries simultaneously, or select the ones you want to search. More than two million words now indexed.—cl

Bibliographies
See *Webliography of Science and Technology Metasites*

Abstracts and Indexes
Social Sciences Research Network
www.SSRN.Com/
Publishes abstracts from published and pre-published journal articles in the social sciences. Searchable by title, author, and journal title.

Table of Contents Services
UnCover
http://uncweb.carl.org/
Contents information of 18,000 journal titles. There is free access to the UnCover database to look at citations. Faxed, e-mail, or postal document delivery is fee-based.

Key Primary Documents
(annual reports, law codes, and statistical sources)

United States Census Information
This is the summary data, not the detailed individual data, needed by genealogists or historians.

PHYSICAL SCIENCES:
Directories
The Internet Library Directory of Science and Technology Associations
www.ipl.org/cgi-bin/ref/aon.out.pl?id=sci0000
Provides links to hundreds of Association Websites.

The Thomas Register of American Manufacturers
www.thomasregister.com/
The online version of a reference classic. Requires free online registration which then gives you access to: ability to search 155,000 companies, 60,000 product, and service classification headings, and 124,000 brand names; modify search results by selected states and by detailed product descriptions; gain easy access to 5,500 online supplier catalogs, 1,000-plus company Websites, and receive detailed Literature by Fax from over 1,000 companies at no cost; purchase line item products through the electronic commerce.—TPN Register (TPN)

Dictionaries
Eric's Treasure Troves of Science
www.treasure-troves.com/
Entries can be searched by keyword or browsed by the following categories: astronomy, biography, books, chemistry, life, math, music, or physics. Each category includes hundreds of terms, many well referenced.

OneLook Dictionaries, The Faster Finder
www.onelook.com/
The ultimate Internet dictionary lookup site. Search 475 general and specialized English dictionaries simultaneously, or select the ones you want to search. More than two million words now indexed.—[Annotation from LII]

Bibliographies
See *Webliography of Science and Technology Metasites*

Abstracts and Indexes
National Technical Information Service (NTIS)
www.ntis.gov/search.htm
Free searching of keywords in titles only. Results provide title, personal author, corporate author, NTIS number, cost, and pagination of document. Online ordering is available. Full searching is fee based.

Northern Light
www.northernlight.com/search.html
Search free Websites as well as proprietary news sources. By limiting a news search on Northern Light to the "Special Collection" database, one can search proprietary publications. The searching is free. The full text of fee-based articles can be ordered and viewed online often for as little as $1.00 per article. The "Special Edition" section provides in-depth coverage of major news stories. The "Special Collection" is a unique combination of premium data representing over 5,400 journals, books, magazines, databases, and newswires not easily found on the World Wide Web.

Table of Contents Services
Elsevier Contents Direct
www.elsevier.nl/homepage/alert.htt?mode=direct
A free e-mail service which delivers Elsevier Science book and journal tables of contents directly to your PC, providing you with the very latest information on soon-to-be published research.

Elsevier Contents Search
www.elsevier.nl/homepage/alert.htt?mode= contents&main
Provides online tables of contents for more than 1,100 Elsevier Science journals, and author index and keyword search facilities, plus journal volumes and issues listed per year.

UnCover
http://uncweb.carl.org/
Contents information of 18,000 journal titles. There is free access to the UnCover database to look at citations. Faxed, e-mail, or postal document delivery is fee-based.

Encyclopedias
How Stuff Works
www.howstuffworks.com/
Dozens and dozens of articles clearly written on how various technologies in the world around us work.

Information Please: Online Dictionary, Internet Encyclopedia & Almanac Reference
www.infoplease.com/
Searchable collection of science and technology information in online almanacs, dictionaries, and the *5th Edition Columbia Encyclopedia* online.

Tech Encyclopedia
www.techweb.com/encyclopedia/
Over 11,000 technology terms are included. Provides lengthy definitions, some articles have pictures available for free. Sometimes provides Web links. Lists terms that appear alphabetically before and after the search term.

E-serials
American Heritage of Invention and Technology
www.americanheritage.com/i&t/
The stories of people, machines, and ideas that have brought us to our present degree of mastery is part of the mission of this publication. The online version offers full-text access to selected articles and abstracts of others only available in print.

New Scientist
www.newscientist.com/home.html
Most articles are available full text going back to April 1997. Includes special reports and features not available in print on topics such as marijuana, artificial intelligence, animal experimentation, and more. Also includes job listings, editorials, reviews, and letters.

Popular Science
www.popsci.com/
Full-text access to news and feature stories, as well as links to interesting science Websites.

News (Current Events)
ScienceDaily
www.sciencedaily.com/
A free, advertising-supported online magazine that brings you breaking news about the latest discoveries and hottest research projects in everything from astrophysics to zoology. The magazine's articles are actually news releases submitted by leading universities and other research organizations around the world. It is updated daily.

TechWeb
www.techweb.com/
The technology news site. Gives top stories for the day, the week, free feature stories, and stories by major news categories. Also provides stories on stocks and technology stock quotes.

Key Primary Documents (annual reports, law codes, statistical sources)
Internet Public Library: Calculation & Conversion Tools Reference
www.ipl.org/ref/RR/static/ref1300.html
There are so many options for conversion resources that it is hard to pick the quintessential site. IPL has listed and described the differences of many sites quite nicely.

USPTO Patent Databases
www.uspto.gov/patft/index.html
The U.S. Patent and Trademark Office (PTO) now offers Web access to bibliographic and full-text patent databases, covering January 1, 1976, to the most recent weekly issue date.

E-library Builder Stories

INFOMINE Scholarly Internet Resource Collections

University of California, Riverside, California, USA
http://infomine.ucr.edu
http://infomine.ucop.edu
http://lib-www.ucr.edu
Contact: Steve Mitchell, smitch@ucrac1.ucr.edu

INFOMINE is both an Internet resource-finding tool and a collection-development tool. It helps students, faculty, researchers, and information professionals find important educational and academic resources quickly. At the same time, it also helps to simplify the Internet resource collection process for librarians anywhere in the world who are developing e-libraries, or instructors who are trying to incorporate Internet resources into their courses. According to INFOMINE staff:

> We currently have over 15,000 records in most major academic disciplines and, during 1998, supported over 660,000 search sessions (averaging five searches each). According to Alta Vista, over 6,000 other Web pages link to us (a large majority are from institutions of higher education).

INFOMINE was initiated by Steve Mitchell, science reference librarian, and Margaret Mooney, head of the Government Publications Department of the Library of the University of California, Riverside during the winter1993–1994.

At first, INFOMINE was supported by a small team of, primarily, line librarians who saw the value of the Web and the role librarians could play in providing a serious finding tool for important scholarly and educational resources. As the concept continued to prove its value, our Library Administration enthusiastically endorsed it.

No collection plan was written for INFOMINE but the goals were clear to the librarians involved. Employing their in-depth training as subject bibliographers and selectors, they have worked together to:

> . . . provide a useful, high quality Internet finding tool for academics and university-level students and others both within and outside the University of California; demonstrate the value of the Internet to faculty, students, and librarians; and explore new roles and services for academic librarians and libraries in the Internet Age. An adjunct goal has been to work together across campus boundaries to reduce the need for librarians at all campuses to create redundant finding tools at great expense in terms of Full Time Equivalency (FTE) and which overlap greatly in content.

INFOMINE was conceived as a Web-based e-library from its inception. It was one of the very first e-libraries on the Web.

> We wanted to create a librarian-built project that was of, by, and for the Web in order to demonstrate to our profession and others that we could make major contributions in this environment and that, conversely, this environment was going to become extremely important to us and our users.

Briefly, in 1995, the INFOMINE creators considered distributing the library collection via CD-ROM or print but felt that these distribution mechanisms would be outdated too quickly to be useful. Production of CD-ROM or print versions would also take time and effort away from the main Web-based e-library.

INFOMINE was originally run on a 486 PC running Linux and the Apache Webserver software. As INFOMINE usage grew, the system migrated to a cluster of fast Pentiums and a Sun workstation at different locations around the University of California. They are using mSQL as their Web database management system, but plan to redesign for the Sybase dbms soon.

Start-up costs for equipment and software were minimal as much of the hardware was already available at the University and the software was free or low cost.

> The system is pretty simple . . . We also had the benefit of very talented student programmers. I'd have to guess at the amount, but it was probably under $15,000 to be up and running reasonably well the first year. Twelve thousand or so of the $15,000 could be attributed to our programmer's time and the time of volunteer librarians contributing to the resource . . . at least for 1994.

Mitchell and Mooney worked with the student programmers to build the INFOMINE Web-based e-library. For the most part, they were self-taught, as they wanted to do things with INFOMINE that had not been done before. They also developed new collecting and indexing routines and training support materials for the librarians who collected the Internet resources for the project.

> For the first year or two we "learned" and progressed by inventing much of what we needed to do. For instance, we were among the first to couple a database with the Web (we learned we were doing "CGI" after we had done it); we were among the first to have dynamic HTML search results pages; we were among the first to hyperlink our indexing terminology; we were among the very first to apply LCSH, in a very streamlined (i.e. "core") way, to Web resources. Contributors, the majority being UC public services librarians, have taken their skills in searching databases (and therefore knowing the ins and outs of database structures), their skills in collecting worthwhile print resources, and their skills in using LCSH and have amalgamated these in doing their INFOMINE work. The point here is that librarian skills have easily transferred to the Internet and training requirements in most cases have been minimal (an hour or two intensive—often over the phone—followed by a few hours of indirect supervision on the part of the facilitator/editor of the particular INFOMINE file). We, of course, have also done several group training sessions at various campuses.

The team of resource collecting coordinators for each subject area are:

Government Information:
   Lynne Reasoner (government publications librarian, UCR)
Visual and Performing Arts:
   Lorelei Tanji (arts bibliographer, UC Irvine)
Physical Sciences :
   Fred Yuengling (science reference librarian and physical sciences selector, UC Santa Cruz)

Biology, Agriculture, and Medicine, Internet Enabling Tools and Instructional Resources:
Steve Mitchell (science reference librarian)
Instructional Resources K-12:
Julie Mason (Outreach Coordinator, UCR)
Maps/GIS INFOMINE:
Wendie Helms (maps collection curator, UCR)
Social Sciences/Humanities Coalition of ALA groups, Ethnic Resources:
Pat Flowers (reference librarian, UCR)

With the exception of our half-time programmer position, INFOMINE contributors aren't so much designees as volunteers who see the need to do this service. As UC librarians, as in many other institutions, we get a certain amount of credit for research and authorship. So, INFOMINE participation brings credit in these areas and service to our clientele.

These librarians incorporate INFOMINE resources collection activities into their usual collection responsibilities within their subject areas for print and other electronic resources.

We see the extension of these skills and responsibilities to online resources on the Internet as a natural and evolving part of what we should be doing anyway. And, by working together, as mentioned, using INFOMINE as a centralized collection tool, we reduce the significant expenditures in FTE that would otherwise occur across the system if each campus created its own version of INFOMINE or added solely to their increasingly Webbed, but campus-specific, OPACs.

Over 20 UC librarians from eight UC campuses and other universities and colleges participate in collecting resources for INFOMINE. The project has support from the government librarians group of UC, the Western Association of Map Librarians, GARLIC (a group of UC, Getty, USC, and other academic librarians in the arts), Reforma, and the American Indian Library Association, among many others.

Some of these librarians contribute up to 30 percent of their working time to INFOMINE collection activities. Others contribute only occasionally.

About one quarter of us are frequent contributors; one half are consistent contributors; one quarter are occasional contributors.

The INFOMINE coordinators are working to expand the number of contributors in the future.

> We feel that, while other academic finding tools have been built on a campus-by-campus basis, many are coming to discover that serious, consistent work is involved, that content overlap with INFOMINE is significant, and that by working together we may be able to pool our resources and efforts more effectively.

Plans are underway to improve the searching and display functions, as well as to reorganize and improve the database. Version 3, which will incorporate these changes in addition to improving overall performance, was to be released in March 1999.

Longer-range work in augmenting the INFOMINE e-library approach with that of an academically focused Web search engine is occurring via a joint, three-year INFOMINE/UC Riverside Computer Science Department project. Related, semi-automated routines for finding, adding, and editing resources, as well as collection maintenance, are being developed. The project has been made possible through $300,000 of funding provided by the Fund for the Improvement of Post-secondary Education, U.S. Department of Education.

Ongoing developments are managed cooperatively by "Margaret and Steve together with Carlos Rodriguez (science reference librarian and HTML development coordinator, UCR), our programmers, UC Riverside Computer Science Department faculty, grad students, and the coordinators and contributors of each subject INFOMINE. All work together with our users to bring forward new ideas."

Individuals, libraries, or other organizations interested in working on INFOMINE should contact Steve Mitchell. See also:

Mitchell, S. and Mooney, M. 1996. "INFOMINE A Model Web-based Academic Virtual Library. *Information Technology and Libraries* (http://infomine.ucr.edu/pubs/italmine.html)

> It is important to note in ending that many of us who directly provide Internet access to faculty and students have found that expectations for robotic and other Internet navigational or finding tools which provide very minimal human input have not been met. In comparison, the INFOMINE virtual library is an efficient and academically focused organizing tool which joins the vast, traditional experience of our profession in organizing information with the Internet in order to help create intelligent order among and access to high-quality, well-selected, and annotated electronic resources. (p. 5).

Scholarly Internet Resource Collections

About INFOMINE   *University of California*

Version 3.1 Introduced! | New Resources Alert Service

New! Multiple Database Searching

Electronic Journals

Biological, Agricultural & Medical Sciences

Government Information

Instructional Resources: K-12

Instructional Resources: University

Internet Enabling Tools (Help, HTML, Finding Tools...)

Maps & GIS

Physical Sciences, Engineering, Computing & Math

Social Sciences & Humanities (Reference, Business, Literature...)

Visual & Performing Arts

[California Digital Library]
[General Reference | MELVYL ® Catalog | Search/Finding Tools]
[UC Campuses/Libraries/People | News Resources | E-Journal Guides]
[Libraries Worldwide | Carl UnCover | Suggest a Resource | Comments]

INFOMINE Scholarly Internet Resource Collection

Cyberstacks

Iowa State University Ames, Iowa, USA
www.public.iastate.edu/~CYBERSTACKS/
Contact: Gerry McKiernan, gerrymck@iastate.edu

CyberStacks(sm) was initiated in 1995 by Gerry McKiernan as part of a research project within the Iowa State University Library where librarians with faculty status are expected to engage in research and to contribute to the scholarly literature. The CyberStacks(sm) project was conceived with two factors in mind:

> The first was interest in supplementing and augmenting access to our local print reference collection that had recently been extensively weeded. The vision here was to provide distributed access to a biological sciences reference collection, not just on-site access that has been the case. I also had an interest in augmenting this collection with additional titles of *potential* reference value that would not have been selected in print due to their specialized nature.
>
> The second major factor was the perceived inadequacies and limitations of then current search engines and early efforts to organize access to Web and other Net resources. CyberStacks(sm) was created as a prototype demonstration service to facilitate access to selected Internet and World Wide Web (WWW) resources in biological sciences through a comprehensive application of the Library of Congress Classification Schedules, a well-established structure and scheme that has been used by research libraries for organizing information sources for generations.

CyberStacks (sm) began as a prototype demonstration service. There was no written collection plan other than the two factors explained above.

> CyberStacks(sm) was initially viewed as a project to explore the use of an established library classification scheme to facilitate access to selected WWW resources by current staff and potential clientele of the biological sciences section of the Reference and Instructional Services of the Iowa State University Library, Ames, Iowa.

The project was intended from the beginning to be a Web-based e-library, organized within the structures of traditional library materials cataloging and classification.

McKiernan created the CyberStacks(sm) Web-based e-library on library PCs and published it on the Iowa State University's UNIX Web-server. HTML coding was originally done directly with the library PCs logged onto the UNIX system using the UNIX editors and published directly into the UNIX Web-server. This method proved to be tedious and time-consuming as the project grew. In December 1995, McKiernan received research funding to support a graduate student assistant. Together they learned how to use the directly-connected DEC 3000 UNIX workstations located in public computer labs.

> The UNIX workstation with its ability to establish several separate sessions, to copy and paste text and graphics, to establish multiple Netscape sessions, and to process data more readily, would prove to be ideal for the next phase of our project.

(See: "Casting the Net: The Development of a Resource Collection for an Internet Database _Untangling the Web" www.library.ucsb.edu/untangle/mckiernan.html).

Although the project uses Iowa State University computer hardware and software, McKiernan also leases an additional 50 megabytes of disk storage space for CyberStacks(sm) and some of his other Web clearinghouses. The total direct cost is about $40 a year. There was no cost to the Iowa State University Libraries because work on the project was performed on McKiernan's personal or regular vacation time.

> In the beginning, CyberStacks(sm) was, for the most part, a one-person research project, with much of the initial effort performed on personal time—time I've devoted to CyberStacks(sm) has varied since it was formally established in November 1995. During our vacation break in December 1995 and January 1996, I spent more than 12 hours a day in seven-day weeks for six weeks on the project. Later, the time averaged about 20–25 hours a week on CyberStacks(sm)-related matters. Currently, I spend about one to two hours per week for perfunctory updates.

Other Iowa State University librarians and library clients are given opportunities to nominate titles for consideration, but Gerry McKiernan has the overall responsibility for updating and maintaining the e-library collection.

Two graduate student assistants have assisted in the collection and technical maintenance. They were paid for by a research grant received from the Iowa State University's Committee on International Programs and from an ISU library's research incentive fund.

> With funds provided this program we were able to undertake a systematic review Web resources that relate the mission of two interna-

tional research centers at Iowa State. While most of the current collection consists of reference works, funding from this grant made it possible to expand the scope of the CyberStacks(sm) collection to include journal tables of contents, selected full-text serial titles, and non-reference monographic works, with subject coverage relevant to the interests of these centers—in addition, significant studies, essays, reports, proceedings, or other unique information provide sources of potential value to these programs.

Personnel were selected, trained, and supervised by McKiernan:

> While the university's server did not permit the processing of CGI scripts for forms, a basic template could be created in HTML to facilitate the selection and preliminary incorporation of candidate resources. As we seek not to analyze a resource but to characterize it in a manner that permits the user to judge its potential usefulness, the template format was simple, consisting of three major divisions—a resource title and URL field, a Summary section, and a To Search section. The Summary section consists of three duplicate HTML blockquote fields, while the To Search section consists of two. Although we have not sought to standardize the format of the data provided for each selected resource within CyberStacks(sm), an effort has been made to include excerpted information from the source itself that describes its subject coverage, scope, size, and/or record structure, as well as available special features or functions.
>
> Using our established template, personnel were instructed to visit a site and to prepare a profile that would characterize a resource, which subsequently was reviewed by me.

Future plans include review of the entire collection to identify broken links, site updates, and add select significant potential candidates to its title index.

CyberStacks(sm) Main Main

Select A Subject Group

G	Geography, Anthropology and Recreation	
H	Social Sciences	
J	Political Science	
K	Law	
Q	Science	
R	Medicine	
S	Agriculture	
T	Technology	
U	Military Science	
V	Naval Science	

CyberStacks(sm)

Cyberstacks

Print and Electronic Publications Cited or Consulted in Chapter Six

Durusau P. 1998. *High Places in Cyberspace : A Guide to Biblical and Religious Studies, Classics, and Archaeological Resources on the Internet* (2nd Ed.) Atlanta: Scholars Press.

Ferrante, J. M. 1997. *Sociology.Net : Sociology on the Internet.* Belmont, Calif.: Wadsworth Pub Co.

Grant, G. B. and Grobman, L. M. 1998. *The Social Worker's Internet Handbook.* Harrisburg, Pa.: White Hat Communications.

He, J. 1998. *Internet Resources for Engineers : A Practical Handbook for Students.* Oxford: Butterworth-Heinemann.

McGeachin, Robert B. 1998. "Selection Criteria for Web-Based Resources in a Science and Technology Library Collection." *Issues in Bio-sciences Librarianship* (www.library.ucsb.edu/istl/98–spring/article2.html).

McKiernan. G. 1996. "Casting the Net: The Development of a Resource Collection for an Internet Database _Untangling the Web" (www.library.ucsb.edu/untangle/mckiernan.html).

Mitchell, S. and Mooney, M. 1996. "INFOMINE A Model Web-based Academic Virtual Library," *Information Technology and Libraries* (http://infomine.ucr.edu/pubs/italmine.html).

Partin, R. L. 1998. *Prentice Hall Directory of Online Social Studies Resources.* New York: Prentice Hall Trade.

Smagula, C.S. 1997. *BioInformation on the World Wide Web 1997: An Annotated Directory of Molecular Biology Tools, 2nd Ed.* Dallas, Texas: BIOTA Publications.

Thomas, B. 1997–98. *The Internet for Scientists and Engineers.* Bellingham, WA: SPIE-The International Society for Optical Engineering (www.spie.org/pm61/).

Webliographies Included with Chapter Six

Biological Science, Social and Physical Sciences, and Technology Resource Metasites

Biological:
Agriculture Network Information Center (AgNIC)
www.agnic.org/
Contact: Agnic@agnic.org
A distributed network that provides access to agriculture-related information, subject area experts, and other resources.

Ann Marie Malley's Biomedical and Life Sciences Sites
www.calacademy.org/research/library/biodiv/biblio/sla98.htm

Bioscience Resources on the Internet
www.emile-21.com/BRI/welcome.html
Contact: bri-prospective-request@linux.it
Four-week research training course.

BIOSCL – Electronic Newsgroup Network for Biology
www.bio.net
Contact: BIOSCI Administrator, biosci-help@net.bio.net
Not only is this a "no fee" communications forum, this also contains a metasite for all categories of bioscience.

CSU Browser
http://arnica.csustan.edu/
Contact: Steve Wolf, swolf@arnica.csustan.edu
Search 36 categories relating to bioscience—from agricultural science to zoology.

Doing Biological Research on the Internet
http://www-de.gnacademy.org/netbio/dbri/
This four-week course provides hands-on experience on Website building, moo use, and research collaboration.

Envirolink
www.envirolink.org/
Contact: EnviroLink Network, support@envirolink.org
Extensive links to environmental sites along with a chat room, job center, and more.

INFOMINE – Comprehensive Biological, Agricultural, & Medical Internet Resource Collection
http://lib-www.ucr.edu/bioag/
Contact: Steve Mitchell, smitch@ucrac1.ucr.edu
Large annotated collection of Internet resources related to biology, agriculture, and medicine. Resources have been determined to be "of use" as a scholarly information resource in research or educational activities at the university level.

Internet Biologist
http://emile-21.com/NetBio/welcome.html
Contact: webmaster@emile-21.com
Fosters virtual connections between biologists at disparate locations, provides training opportunities for research scientists with the integration of Internet tools into their research, and provides networking and mentoring opportunities for the international biological research community.

Not Just Cows
www.morrisville.edu/~drewwe/njc/
Contact: Bill Drew, drewwe@MORRISVILLE.EDU
Guide to agriculture and agricultural resources on the Internet.

The Finger Searcher Science Seeker Newsletter
www.connect.ab.ca/~xdr/fsearch/fsindex.html
Contact: Martin H. Badke, martinb@connect.ab.ca
Weekly newsletter of science and science education resources (search tools, teacher resources, and all areas of science).

SciCentral
http://scicentral.com
Contact: scicentral@scicentral.com
This metadatabase includes all areas of science and their subcategories with directories, research, and latest news.

Web Spinning
www.davincipress.com/webspinning.html
Contact: Kevin Ahern, kevin@davincipress.com
Online version of print column published in *Genetic Engineering News* which reviews Websites for biotechnology and bioengineering.

Social Science:
Administration of Justice Guide – George Mason University Library
http://library.gmu.edu/resources/socsci/criminal.html
Contact: Kimberly C. Kowal, kkowal@osf1.gmu.edu
Provides links to indexes and abstracts, topical guides, statistics, legal resources, law enforcement, organizations, electronic lists, and jobs. This site won an Argus award for its good organization, description of resources, and quality of sites.

American Studies Web: Reference and Research
www.georgetown.edu/crossroads/asw/index.html
Contact: cepacs@gusun.georgetown.edu
Includes links to sites about: economy and politics, gender and sexuality, historical and archival resources, philosophy and religion, race and ethnicity, sociology and demographics, and more. Maintained by the American Studies Crossroads Project, sponsored by the American Studies Association, and funded with major grants from the U.S. Department of Education and the Annenberg/CPB Project.

Archaeology on the Net
www.serve.com/archaeology/
Contact: archaeology@mail.serve.com
A highly commercial, yet comprehensive, venture that links to Websites, journals, and organizations; provides a list and archived list of new books; easy searching of amazon.com for relevant topics; and hosts ArchPub, a mailing list for keeping up with publications in the fields.

Argos – Limited Area Search of the Ancient and Medieval Internet
http://argos.evansville.edu/
Contact: Anthony F. Beavers, tb2@evansville.edu
Argos is the first peer-reviewed, limited area search engine (LASE) on the World Wide Web. It has been designed to cover the ancient and medieval worlds. Sites included have been selected by editors who look for sites of academic and scholarly quality.

Argus Clearinghouse – Social Science and Social Issues
www.clearinghouse.net/cgi-bin/chadmin/viewcat/
Social_Sciences___Social_Issues?kywd++
Contact: Argus Associates, Inc., clearinghouse@argus-inc.com
Collects and rates the metasites. Subheadings include, anthropology, archaeology, communities and urban planning, families, linguistics, political science, psychology, social activism, social issues, and sociology. Not comprehensive, but the rating system is unique.

Arts and Humanities Data Service
http://AHDS.AC.UK/
Contact: Daniel Greenstein, Director; Daniel.Greenstein@ahds.ac.uk or info@ahds.ac.uk
The gateway provides access to high-quality information providers of data from the disciplines of archaeology, history, literature and language, the performing, and visual arts.

Horus
www.ucr.edu/h-gig/horuslinks.html
Contact: James Seaman, horus@h-gig.ucr.edu
University of California, Riverside's comprehensive database of history Web links.

INFOMINE – Social Sciences and Humanities
http://lib-www.ucr.edu/sshinfo.html
Contact: Nancy Getty, gettyn@ucrac1.ucr.edu
Browsable and searchable index of thousands of sites of use as a scholarly information resource in research or educational activities at the university level.

Philosophy Around the Web
http://users.ox.ac.uk/~worc0337/phil_index.html
Contact: Peter King, peter.king@philosophy.ox.ac.uk
Humorous site with 12 main categories of philosophy databases (organizations, papers, philosophers, education, etc.).

Philosophy in Cyberspace
http://www-personal.monash.edu.au/~dey/phil/
Contact: Dey Alexander, dey@silas.cc.monash.edu.au
Section one lists branches of philosophy with links to sites for each; section two contains links to books, journals, library, and other text related information; section three lists organizations such as academic institutions, associations, centers, etc; section four lists forums, newsgroups, etc.; and finally, section five includes a miscellany of jobs, humor, conferences, etc. Thousands of entries, and a link to Hippias, a search engine of WWW philosophy sites.

Political Resources on the Net
www.agora.stm.it/politic/
Contact: Roberto Cicciomessere, r.cicciomessere@agora.it
Listings of political sites available on the Internet sorted by country, with links to parties, organizations, governments, media, and more, from all around the world.

SocioSite – Subject Areas
www.pscw.uva.nl/sociosite/TOPICS/index.html
Contact: Albert Benschop, benschop@pscw.uva.nl
Created in the Netherlands, this site has a European emphasis on sites, but has an extensive listing of subjects and sites covered.

Voice of the Shuttle Humanities Research
http://vos.ucsb.edu
Contact: Alan Liu, ayliu@humanitas.ucsb.edu
Huge source of resources of all humanities topics and their subcategories: art, language, politics, culture, religion, etc.

Women's Studies/Women's Issues Resource Sites
http://www-unix.umbc.edu/~korenman/wmst/links.html
Contact: Joan Korenman, korenman@umbc2.umbc.edu
From the founder of WMST-L, one of the first electronic forums for women, comes this comprehensive site which is a selective, alphabetical listing of Websites containing resources and information about women's studies/women's issues, with an emphasis on sites of particular use to an academic women's studies program.

Physical Science and Technology:
A Guide to the Web for Statisticians
http://maths.uq.oz.au/~gks/webguide/
Contact: Gordon Smyth, gks@maths.uq.edu.au
This metasite contains several statistical categories (computing, methodology, journals) and links to other sites.

AstroWeb
www.stsci.edu/science/net-resources.html
Contact: Bob Jackson, jackson@stsci.edu or astroweb@nrao.edu
Exhaustive metasite of astronomy and astrophysics of Internet resources.

The Collection of Computer Science Bibliographies
http://liinwww.ira.uka.de/bibliography/index.html
Contact: Alf-Christian Achilles, achilles@ira.uka.de or liinwwwa@ira.uka.de
Searchable metasite with 16 major computer science topic areas containing over 930,000 references (reports, papers, and articles); 60,000 linked to online versions.

CyberStacks
www.public.iastate.edu/~CYBERSTACKS
Contact: gerrymck@iastate.edu
A centralized, integrated, and unified collection of significant World Wide Web (WWW) and other Internet resources categorized using the Library of Congress classification scheme. This is prototype demonstration service emphasizing the fields of science and technology.

The Edinburgh Engineering Virtual Library (EEVL)
www.eevl.ac.uk/
Contact: webmaster@eevl.icbl.hw.ac.uk
EEVL is the U.K. gateway to engineering information on the Internet, and these 250 sites are taken from the EEVL database that contains details of 3,190 quality engineering resources.

EELS – Engineering Electronic Library Sweden
http://eels.lub.lu.se/
Contact: Kjell Jansson, Project Coordinator; kj@lib.kth.se
or Traugott Koch, Technical Support; Taugott.Koch@ub2.lu.se
or EELS@munin.lub.lu.se
Search this metasite of seven engineering classifications as well as physics and mathematics.

Favorite Internet Resources of an Underemployed Geologist
www.groupz.net/~hoppy/links.htm
Contact: John W. Hopkins; hoppy@groupz.net
Excellent starting resource for earth science and geology. This annotated geological metasite also contains some general information links, too.

The Finger Searcher Science Seeker Newsletter
www.connect.ab.ca/~xdr/fsearch/fsindex.html
Contact: Martin H. Badke, martinb@connect.ab.ca
Weekly newsletter of science and science education resources (search tools, teacher resources, and all areas of science).

The Internet Pilot to Physics (TIPTOP)
http://physicsweb.org/TIPTOP/
Contact: tiptop-user@ioppublishing.com
The world's most comprehensive index to online physics resources, including selected online resources, institutes, and forums.

Issues in Science and Technology Librarianship
www.library.ucsb.edu/istl/
Contact: Andrea L. Duda, Editor; duda@library.ucsb.edu
Quarterly publication which serves as a vehicle for sci-tech librarians to share details of successful programs, materials for the delivery of information services, background information, and opinions on topics of current interest to publish research and bibliographies on issues in science and technology libraries.

Life In the Universe
www.lifeintheuniverse.com/
Contact: Metacreations at arachnid@metacreations.com
The contents of this site accompany the Stephen Hawking's *Life in the Universe* CD-ROM. Here you will find links to scientific Websites as well as information relating subjects such as the Big Bang, continental shift, black holes, etc. The site claims that new items, such as chats and threaded discussions will be added periodically.

Math Archives
http://archives.math.utk.edu
Contact: help@archives.math.utk.edu
Searchable metasite of teaching materials for all areas and grade levels, archives and links to other math sites.

The Math Forum Internet Mathematics Library
http://forum.swarthmore.edu/library/
Contact: The Math Forum, webmaster@forum.swarthmore.edu
With hundreds of links to mathematics Internet sites, this project of the Math Forum provides one easily navigable location for finding math content on the Web. The sites are organized by mathematics topics, teaching topics, resource types, and education levels.

Networked Computer Science Technical Reference Library (NCSTRL)
www.ncstrl.org/
Contact: help@ncstrl.org
View this international collection of computer science research reports and papers by year, institution, or browse by subject.

The Online Astronomer
http://astronomer.net/
This site is intended for the amateur astronomer who is just getting started and looking for some basic information. Includes lots of links to astronomy sites.

SciCentral
http://scicentral.com
Contact: scicentral@scicentral.com
This metadatabase includes all areas of science and their subcategories with directories, research, and latest news.

STS – Science & Technology Section (of the Association of College and Research Libraries)
www.ALA.org/Acrl/sts/sts.html
Contact: Web Editors, David Atkins, atkins@aztec.lib.utk.edu
or Janet Hughes, jah@psulias.psu.edu
A forum for sci-tech librarians to access, exchange, and impact this type of information; conferences, discussions, publications, and resources.

Sheffield ChemDex
www.chemdex.org/
Contact: Dr. Mark J. Winter, webelements@sheffield.ac.uk
Huge site containing 20 chemistry categories,as well as institutes, companies, links to Websites (in many different languages), software, etc.

StatLab Index
http://lib.stat.cmu.edu
Contact: Pantelis Vlachos, vlachos@stat.cmu.edu
A system for distributing statistical software, datasets, and information by electronic mail, FTP, and WWW.

See **Collection Development Related Discussion Groups, E-serials and Guides, Evaluation Guides, and Workshops** Webliography in Chapter One for discussion lists, newsgroups, e-serials, and other resources cited in this chapter.

7

Collecting Web-based Education, Current Awareness, and Readers' Advisory Information Resources; Web-based Information Resources for Print; and Other Collection Activities

"Using the Internet in education is a global, grassroots phenomenon. Even though governments and major corporations are debating (and in some cases funding) the construction of the information super-highway, thousands of educators, parents, and community members are not waiting but are using what's available now to transform today's classrooms into global learning environments. . . . Learning to harness Internet resources does not require you to become an expert in computers, networking, or advanced technology. The goal is still to create an effective learning environment; the Internet is just a tool to help you to achieve this goal.

The Internet has changed forever the way I teach, and the way my students learn. None of us is willing to ever go back to the way it was before, and we join with thousands of others waiting online to welcome you into this exciting process."

From Serim, F. and Koch, M. (1996) *NetLearning: Why Teachers Use the Internet.* **Sebastopol, CA: O'Reilly, Inc. (p. 4).**

Education, Current Awareness, and Reader's Advisory Internet Resource Collection and Evaluation

Education resources are defined, for discussion in this chapter, as resources which support the work of students and provide practical support for teachers. In fact, another way of stating the working definition of education for this chapter is "homework help." Some higher-education resources are included in the Webliography at the end of this chapter, but the focus will be on K–12 educational support. In the United States we say kindergarten through 12th grade to denote the years before students go to college. Education resources broadly defined could include any of the resources in any of the other chapters in this book. College information resources are also included in this broad definition.

K–12 homework-help information is easy to find on the Internet. As always, the real problem is finding help for specific kinds and age/grade levels of homework. College information consists of Websites provided by colleges, financial aid agencies, and educational organizations. This information includes everything from course and program descriptions and applications, to anecdotal descriptions by current and past students.

Current awareness resources are basically news, weather, entertainment, and sports sources. Current awareness resources that have never been available in the past, are now available on the Internet. For example, we can get transcripts of CNN breaking news (www.cnn.com), play-by-play baseball games at ESPN Sports Zone (www.espnsportszone.com/), and celebrities from Usher to Riverdance maintain Web pages with their current information. The weather (www.weather.com) was one of the first current awareness resources to be made available through the Internet. Whenever I travel, I check the weather report for where I'm going by connecting to the weather.com site.

Reader's advisory and print collection development information resources are two sides of the same coin. Reader's advisory tools are the resources we use to help us recommend books to our clients that they may want to read for educational, recreational, or other reasons. Print collection development tools are the resources we use to decide which books to acquire and include in the library collection to serve our clients' educational, recreation, and other information needs. These same tools can be used for the collection of books, videos, and other locally held materials for our libraries.

The Internet Education Information Resource Collection Plan

What Purpose Will Your Web-based E-library Education Collection Serve? What Subjects Will be Covered? For Whom are You Collecting Education-related Internet Resources?

Educational resources at the college or university level can literally be any information resource in any subject area. Each school or public librarian simply needs to collect the resources that will be useful to students studying the subjects taught in their schools. Another step must be taken to determine the age-appropriateness of the information resource. For example, it is easy to find the answer to the question what is "warm bloodedness" in mammals. It is a different matter to find an explanation that is meaningful to a younger child. Academic libraries may want to collect these kinds of education resources in their e-libraries to support teacher education in their colleges and universities. The student teachers will benefit from awareness of the resources available to their future students in learning to plan instruction and teach.

What Types of Education-related Internet Resources Will You Link to Through Your E-library?

Education-related Internet reference tools take forms that can be described in terms of traditional reference source types. An annotated Education Core Internet Ready-Reference Collection at the end of this section lists essential Internet reference tools organized by the following reference source types, many of which are also part of any ready-reference collection:

1. Directories of schools, colleges, universities, educational organizations, and programs.
2. Dictionaries of any kind.
3. Abstracts, indexes, and table of contents services for education-related serials. UnCover provides table of contents access to nearly all the major education serials including *Educational Research, High School Journal, Journal of Adult Education, Journal of Education, Reading Research Quarterly*, and *Teacher Education and Practice*.
4. Encyclopedias of any kind.
5. Education e-serials.
6. Bibliographies of educational information sources (see Education Metasites Webliography).
7. Education news or any news site.
8. Special teacher interactive sites such as "Ask Dr. Math" (http://forum.swarthmore.edu/dr.math/) where teachers work interactively with students to help them with homework questions.

How Will You Organize Your Internet Education Resources?

Educational resources can obviously be organized by subject, but also consider organizing them by age appropriateness and/or educational level of the intended client groups.

Identifying and Collecting Internet Education Information Resources

Websites Which Review and Evaluate Internet Resources: Other E-libraries, Subject Collection Guides/Webliographies, Etc.

The first place to look for education-related resources is in other people's e-libraries or directories of resources. Education resource metasites are included in the Webliography for this chapter. There are several really excellent education metasites including "Yahooligans!" (www.yahooligans.com/)—Yahoo!'s special collection of homework and recreational Websites for kids. Other excellent metasites include the OPLIN Website's "OH! Kids" product (http://oplin.lib.oh.us/products/oks/) and "The Education Index" (www.education index.com/) which is an annotated collection of evaluated education resources organized by age, educational level, and subject.

The Academic Info site (www.academicinfo.net) is a metasite for higher-education resources.

Discussion Lists and Newsgroups Where Individual Participants Review and Evaluate Internet Resources

The most important Internet educational resources discussion list is LM_NET. This discussion group is for school library media specialists, or any librarian, teacher, or parent who is working with information intended for k–12 students in any format. The focus is, however, on Internet resources, trouble-shooting, software choices and so on for k–12 libraries. Edresource is a discussion of the education resources available that benefit Internet educators (www.egroups.com/list/edresource/). There are numerous additional discussion lists and newsgroups which discuss and review Internet education resources for different age groups, educational levels, and subject areas. You can locate most of them by searching *The Directory of Scholarly and Professional Electronic Conferences* (through www.arl.org/scomm/edir) or The PHOAKS project (www.phoaks.com) to identify more.

E-journals and Newsletters Which Publish Reviews and Evaluations of Education-related Internet Resources

The Internet Scout project's *The Scout Report* (http://scout.cs.wisc.edu/scout/index.html) is the premier source of reviews of education-related Internet resources. Other e-serials which review education-related Internet resources may be identified by searching the NewJour archives (http://gort.ucsd.edu/newjour/)

or the *ARL Directory of Electronic Journals, Newsletters, and Academic Discussion Lists* companion database Website (www.arl.org)

Print Books and Journals Which Review Education-related Internet Resources

Several books are listed in the Print and Electronic Publications Cited in This Chapter at the end of this chapter. Most of these are actually tutorials, or project manuals for teachers, which also include annotated lists of educational Websites.

Evaluating Internet Education Information Resources

Education resources vary greatly in content and the authority of the information provider. Some of them are provided by students and others by teachers with varying degrees of expertise. The best strategy to follow is the basic evaluating Internet information resources described in Chapter One. When evaluating educational resources related to business, medical, or legal subjects use the strategies for evaluating those types of information described in Chapters Three, Four, and Five, respectively.

Selecting a Core Internet Education Ready-reference Collection

Selection criteria for education-related information resources are derived from the answers arrived at during the collection-planning process. The access, design, and content criteria for assessing the value of Websites for library users are reproduced in Table 7.1. The Education Core Internet Ready-Reference Collection included below was compiled with these criteria in mind. The intended client group is very broadly any English-speaking, child or adult who might be interested in homework help, educational placement information, or scholarship information. The access and design of all these core education-oriented reference Internet resources are based on standards of simplicity and international Internet Web browser compatibility with no special software required for access. All of them are free of direct cost. Archival access is varied in these resources.

Table 7.1   Content Criteria for Internet Resources

Selection Adapted from Caywood (1996) (http://www6.pilot.infi.net/~carolyn/criteria.html)

1. Does the resource meet some current awareness related information need of the e-library's intended clients?
2. Does the resource provide the information at a level and language suitable to the age, educational background, and subject interests of the e-library's intended clients?
3. Does the resource provide information in a form that you want to include in your e-library? News services or e-serials, for example.

Other Selection Criteria Specific to Internet Resources Are:

4. Access and Design
   Will the e-library's intended clients have the computer equipment and software needed to use the resource? Does the resource allow for access by disabled individuals who may need to use text-to-voice software or other enabling tool? Does the resource display in the Web browser within a reasonable amount of time?
5. Archiving
   Will the information provider provide "back issues" or archives of the resource? Will you need to make arrangements to store such information locally if needed? This is especially important in the case of e-serials or current information that will become valuable historical information over time. Most social sciences research information will require some kind of archiving arrangements be made. It doesn't really matter if the information is archived in print publications, backed up to CD-ROM, magnetic tape or other electronic storage media, or simply kept available on the Web for an indeterminate period as long as researchers are assured that it will be archived and available in the future.
6. Cost/Licensing/User Access Control
   Some Internet accessible resources are fee-based. If that is the case, for example as with the *Encyclopedia Britannica* online, consideration will need to be made for not only the cost of the resource, but any licensing arrangements or user access control that must be exercised. For example, will the resource only be accessible by users from within the library's domain or can any library user from any location by using a login and password or library card number access the resource.

Education Core Internet Ready-reference Collection

(See also the Core Internet Ready-reference Collections in Chapters Two–Five)

Directories

American School Directory
www.asd.com/
The Internet guide to all 108,000 k–12 schools in the U.S. Providing information about enrollment, administration, contacts, number of homerooms, type of school, mascot, colors, history, and technology capabilities. Provides links to school homepages when available.

Peterson's Guide Online
www.petersons.com/
Calling itself "the education supersite," Peterson's offers free searching of school and program information from grade school through graduate studies with special subjects such as college choice for African Americans, summer camps and programs, study abroad programs, and lots more. Basic information including contact numbers and addresses is offered for free on all programs, with reference to the print Peterson publication containing full information.

Dictionaries

AltaVista/BabelFish Machine Translation
http://babelfish.altavista.com/cgi-bin/translate?
Use this site like a dictionary to look up words in French, German, Italian, Portuguese, or Spanish and translate them into English, or vice versa.

OneLook Dictionaries, The Faster Finder
www.onelook.com/
The ultimate Internet dictionary lookup site. Search 475 general and specialized English dictionaries simultaneously, or select the ones you want to search. More than two million words now indexed.—[Annotation from LII]

Web of Online Dictionaries
www.Facstuff.bucknell.edu/rbeard/diction.html
While this site does not provide a search across all dictionaries, it is a nice listing of high-quality online dictionaries and has a section of specialized dictionaries in English. Under education, several titles can be found that are not included in OneLook Dictionaries.

Bibliographies

See *Webliography of Education Resource Metasites*

Abstracts, Indexes, and Table of Contents Services

ERIC

http://ericir.syr.edu/Eric/

This version of the ERIC Database provides access to ERIC Document citations from 1966 and ERIC Journal citations from 1966. Updates are about to the previous three to four months.

Northern Light

www.northernlight.com/search.html

By limiting an education search on Northern Light to the "Special Collection" database, one can search popular and scholarly publications. The searching is free. The full text can be ordered and viewed online often for as little as $1.00 per article. The Special Collection is a unique combination of premium data representing over 5,400 journals, books, magazines, databases, and newswires not easily found on the World Wide Web. This includes several journals in the field of education.

UnCover

http://uncweb.carl.org/

Contents information for nearly all the major education serials including *Educational Research*, *High School Journal*, *Journal of Adult Education*, *Journal of Education*, *Reading Research Quarterly*, and *Teacher Education and Practice*. There is free access to the UnCover database to look at citations. Faxed, e-mail, or postal document delivery is fee-based.

Encyclopedias

Encyberpedia

www.encyberpedia.com/ency.htm

Rather than being a resource for educators, it is a resource for students. This encyclopedia is actually a collection of Websites. Some entries lead to full encyclopedic entries, others provide a list of links which subdivide the topic. While in the end it is a bit of a metasite, it does provide an interface that looks encyclopedia-like and is easy for students to use.

History of Education

www.socsci.kun.nl/ped/whp/histeduc/index.html

Here's a site with information for educators about their own craft. Entries fall into several large categories: important people, childhood history, schooling history, themes, schooling USA, and history of educational research. This resource collects full-text entries from all over the Web and presents them in a scholarly and understandable interface. It is also an attractive site to visit.

E-serials
American School Board Journal
www.asbj.com/about.html
Chronicles change, interprets issues, and offers readers—some 40,000 school board members and school administrators—practical advice on a broad range of topics pertinent to school governance and management, student achievement, and the art of school leadership. The online version offers full-text access to some articles, abstracts of some articles, and full table of contents of the print version.

News (Current Events)
Education Week on the Web
www.edweek.org/
Includes the Daily News Section with the best education articles from around the country. Also includes full text of special reports and feature stories.

Chronicle of Higher Education
www.chronicle.merit.edu/
Some free and some fee-based articles. Online subscription accompanies a print subscription. Daily news about higher education with lots of feature stories. A subscription entitles you to daily news reports via email.

Key Primary Documents (annual reports, law codes, and statistical sources)
Education Vital Signs
www.asbj.com/evs/
A publication of the *American School Board Journal,* this site provides annual statistics that evaluate the state of education. Includes statistics such as violence, standards and attainments, indicators of school success, and facts and figures about schools and children.

U.S. Department of Education
www.ed.gov/
Provides access to news on education legislation, loans and student aid information and forms (including FAFSA forms), funding opportunities, statistics from the NCES, and more.

Use the metasites listed in the *Webliography of Education Resource Metasites* to identify "Special teacher interactive sites such as 'Ask Dr. Math' (http://forum.swarthmore.edu/dr.math/) where teachers work interactively with students to help them with homework questions."

The Internet Current Awareness Information Resource Collection Plan

This is one type of information for which the answer is the same for all types of libraries. Everyone—from child to adult—who uses a library—needs current awareness information. A current awareness collection can be very broadly inclusive with listings of newspapers online and access to the online sites of television news services. Or it can be focussed on current awareness in a narrower subject field, such as business, law, or medicine. See Chapters Three–Five for some selected current awareness resources in those subject fields.

News and primary document sources are the real meat of current awareness information. The Internet is without peer in terms of its ability to delivery up-to-the-second news and popular culture information. Primary documents such as live interviews, song lyrics, or photographs are readily available through the Internet.

Current awareness information can be organized in the same structure decided on for the general e-library organization discussed in Chapter One. It could be combined with ready-reference Internet resources as well.

The best place to look for current awareness resources to collect are in other people's e-libraries or directories of resources. Any of the e-libraries listed in any of the subject listings in any of the chapters in this book might help locate useful current awareness resources.

Any discussion list or newsgroup; e-serial; print book; or print serial on any topic might either be a good current awareness information source or point to good current awareness information sources elsewhere on the Internet. See the Collection Development Related Discussion Groups, E-serials and Guides Evaluation Guides and Workshops Webliography in Chapter One for discussion lists, newsgroups, e-serials.

Evaluating Internet Current Awareness Resources

Any current awareness information is only as good as the information provider or new source. The best rule of thumb for evaluating current awareness resources is to look for news organizations that you know and recognize for having a good reputation in researching and publishing news on current events. Use the basic strategies for evaluating Internet resources described in Chapter One to find out who published the information and to verify its currency.

The Internet Reader's Advisory and Print Collection Development Resource Collection Plan

Libraries collect reviews of books, Internet and multi-media resources in order to help both the librarians and the library clients to make choices about specific information sources.

Basically most of these types of Websites are book stores (e.g. Amazon.com (www.amazon.com)), book jobbers (e.g., Baker & Taylor(www.btebis.com/TS2/)) or book publisher store fronts(e.g., Neal-Schuman (www.neal-schuman.com/)). Some are e-serials which publish book reviews, written by librarians or other readers. In her May 1999 "Internet Librarian" column, Karen Schneider writes "Let Your Fingers Do the Collection Development Online," in which she reviews two, free, reader's advisory and print collection development Websites—Bookbrowser: The Guide For Avid Readers (www.bookbrowser.com) and BookFinder.Com (an antiquarian book locator tool; www.bookfinder.com/). She also reviews and finds lacking two fee-based sites published by Baker & Taylor and Ingram.

These types of information are of most use to library staff making recommendations to clients or selecting print materials for acquisitions. The organization of these resources in the e-library should enhance access by library staff. Occasionally, library clients will also want access to reader's advisory related Websites. Tools which are specifically for the selection of reading matter should be placed where library clients will find them easily. For example, you might create a category called "What Books to Read?" which is then sub-organized by non-fiction, fiction, fiction genres, and children's resources.

Publib is a discussion list which, among other useful topics, encourages the sharing and reviewing of materials in all formats of interest to public librarians including specifics and strategies for reader's advisory services. Collection development discussion lists include COLLDV-L, discussion of collection development issues; CONSDIST, discussion of collection and preservation; and ECOLL, discussion of collection development of electronic resources.

Evaluation of reader's advisory and print collection development information is a simple matter. The main criteria will be who is writing the reviews and whether their credentials as a reviewer are acceptable in the context of the kinds of materials being reviewed. These criteria may be discovered about Internet reader's advisory and print collection development information by following the same strategy for evaluating Internet resources used throughout this book and described in Chapter One.

• •

E-library Builder Stories

University of Canterbury Web E-library

University of Canterbury
Christchurch, New Zealand
www.libr.canterbury.ac.nz/
Bronwyn Matthews, b.matthews@libr.canterbury.ac.nz

A librarian working in the Systems Department of the Macmillan Library (Brown, New Zealand Pacific branch) in 1994–95 conceived the idea of creating a "The Library Web Pages." Over time, the project " . . . evolved as individual librarians, particularly those in the Information Services Department, realized that students were wanting to use the Internet for research and were asking about access from the Library."

From the beginning, the project was developed by Information Desk staff with the support of the Systems Department. The library administration tacitly approved the development of the Web-based e-library. The e-library developed within the context of the library beginning to provide training to students in "Basic Web Navigation Using Netscape" in May 1996 and "Search Engines and Subject Searching" later that year.

> In May 1997 an interim Web Management Group (WMG) was set up consisting of the Systems Librarian, Anne Scott, and two associate librarians. Their aim was to work out a management structure for Web work and look at staffing. There was concern that the work that had been done had too much of a central library (humanities, social sciences, and biological sciences) focus, and that the branch libraries on the campus needed to be included. From June 1997, Alison Johnston, the librarian who had done the work to date, was seconded to the Systems Department half-time to work on Web pages. This second segment lasted three months. This librarian (A. Johnston) and the systems librarian went to each branch library (law, engineering, physical sciences, NZ/Pacific) to discuss their needs.

There was no initial written collection plan for the "Library Web Pages" project, but later a document was written, "Policies and Guidelines"(2nd version, Dec. 1996) which describes the collection guidelines and policies.

Very briefly, the creators of the "Library Web Pages" considered publishing them internally on the University of Canterbury campus LAN. The final decision was of course to publish the pages on an Internet-accessible Web server.

The Library purchased a Sun Ultra Enterprise 1 Model 170 running Sun Solaris 2.5.1 to run the Web Server, Silverplatter ERL Server, character and Z39.50 access to the Library catalogue, and a variety of other smaller tasks. It currently has 45GB disk and 256 MB RAM. In the early days, a number of shareware products were used for the Web but we are trying to standardize on Frontpage. FTP Voyager is also used. We have purchased a HP Scanjet 4 to input exam papers, reserve material, etc. Staff have access to PC workstations running OS/2 Warp 3 and now 4, with Netscape 2.02 for OS/2 (runs frames and Java). Staff who are developing Web pages now use NT workstations as we are in the process of moving from OS/2 to NT. Other staff use Word 6 to provide content. Library provides Netscape 3 to users in the library on PCs running Windows 3.11.

Existing personnel within the scope of their regular duties performed all work. Recently, this has become a problem for the members of the WMG. The WMG identified nine staff members who had interest in working on the "Library Web Pages" who have become the Web Working Group (WWG). The original systems librarian—technician/Webmaster is self-taught but is currently taking a course in Website design. The information services librarian, who researched and wrote papers on advanced information storage and retrieval for an MSLIS, took a course on Website design, and desktop publishing. Two other librarians took courses on HTML for librarians. The convener of the WWG (Bronwyn Matthews) attended a one-day commercial seminar on Web design. The WWG members attended the seminar at the University of Canterbury by Roy Tennant in December 1997.

The "Library Web Pages" are supported by a number of staff members. The WMG consists of three senior staff members; the WWG involves nine library staff. These people estimate that they work four to five hours per week on average, the convener six hours.

More work can be done during the university's summer vacation (November–March) than can be done during term-time. There are no formal arrangements about how much time staff can contribute to the work of the WWG—it was added on to their regular duties. However, some were already doing Web-related work as part of those duties.

In the future, their are plans to create the position of a full-time Web manager to coordinate the efforts of those who work on the "Library Web Pages."

Internet Subject Resources

Accountancy
American Studies
Anthropology
Antarctic Information
Art and Architecture
Astronomy
Biochemistry
Chemistry
Chinese
Classics
Computer Science
Economics
Education
Engineering
English
European Union
Feminist Studies

Forestry
French
Geography
Geology
German
History
Humanities
Interdisciplinary Studies
Japanese
Journalism
Law
Library & Information Science
Linguistics
Management
Maori
Mathematics & Statistics
Multidisciplinary Science

Music
New Zealand
Official Publications
Pacific Islands
Philosophy
Physics
Plant and Microbial Science
Political Science
Psychology
Religious Studies
Russian
Social Science
Social Work
Sociology
Speech & Language Therapy
Theatre & Film Studies
Zoology

UNIVERSITY OF CANTERBURY

Library Home

PAC
Library Catalogue

Electronic Resources

Services

Campus Libraries

Staff

Contact Us

SITE MAP
HELP
SEARCH

UNIVERSITY OF CANTERBURY HOME	LIBRARY HOME	PAC	ELECTRONIC RESOURCES	SERVICES
	CAMPUS LIBRARIES	CONTACT US	SEARCH	SITE MAP

Send comments, suggestions and feedback to
webmanager@lib.canterbury.ac.nz
Updated September, 1999

Library
University of Canterbury

University of Canterbury Web E-library

This would make it easier to keep up to date with Web developments, fill out the subjects which are currently not covered by our pages, expand into in-house material such as practice examination papers, restricted loan reprints, online tutorials, etc.; and generally offer our students and staff a comprehensive Website.

Taft Library/Media Center

Marion, Ohio, USA
www.infotaft.marioncity.k12.oh.us/
Contact: Deb Logan
jd3logan@bright.net

Deb Logan built the Taft Library/Media Center e-library to help make the Internet more manageable for the students and teachers of Taft Middle School in Marion, Ohio. Her principal, Mr. Born, felt it was a good idea and encouraged her to build the Taft Library/Media Center Website.

Logan's collection plan was unwritten but simple:

> My primary goal in creating the Taft Library Media Center Website was to create a starting place on the Internet for my students and faculty. In our building, very few individuals have direct experience with the Internet. Also, my middle school students do not have the sophistication to look at information found on the Internet with an adequate level of discrimination. Consequently, I felt that I needed to teach them how to navigate on the "Information Super Highway" and to assist them with locating usable, accurate, and reliable information resources that support the curriculum and/or teach Internet skills. In a manner of speaking, the Taft Library Media Center Website is my method of creating an index to recommended resources for my users. Also, I wanted to make the Internet approachable and attractive for reluctant or uncomfortable users.

She began by collecting lists of recommended sites and organizing them in a notebook by subject and bookmarking sites as she found them. This was over a year before her school had access to the Internet. Since using the lists and bookmarks was cumbersome for her library users, she decided to create a Website containing her collected resources. When the school was connected to the Internet, the e-library was ready for use.

In the library, students and teachers can access the Internet and the e-library on 13 Pentium PCs and a Macintosh. Most of the work building the e-library was done by Logan at home on her personal Pentium PC. The Website is

TAFT* Library Media Center

Taft's Gateway to the World of Information...

This web site is designed to assist students and faculty locate and use electronic information resources. Links are intended to meet basic reference needs and to support the curriculum.

At Taft Middle School information skills are collaboratively taught by the Librarian/Media Specialist and subject teachers in context with the rest of the school's curricula.

***Taft Middle School
Marion, Ohio**

Things to Know about the Internet/ How to Search Links/
Search Engine Links / Reference Tools / Homework Help Links/
Subject Links/ Project Page/ Teacher Resource Links /
Quotations about Books and Reading/
Taft Library Media Policies

Taft Library/Media Center

published on the Web server of one of the three middle schools in Marion, Ohio.

Logan continues to be the only person working directly on the Taft Middle School Library/Media Center's e-library. She learned HTML by taking a workshop and reading books on the topic outside of her regular working hours.

> My primary resource was the class I took at Kent State from Diane Kovacs. I wrote the page in HTML on WordPad. I have several HTML books and class notes that I consulted. The main books that I used were: *HTML 4 for the World Wide Web: Visual QuickStart Guide* (1997) by Elizabeth Castro and *HTML: The Definitive Guide* (1997) by Kennedy, B., Loukides, M., Ed., and Musciano, C.

The costs of the books and training were her only direct costs. She spent considerable amounts of her own personal unpaid time, however, building the e-library. She estimates 500 hours working on the Website. Her library aide assisted with some of the graphics. She is considering student volunteers to help in checking links. Some teachers have also proposed sites and other content ideas. She expects to spend one to four hours per week on maintaining the Website.

The Taft Library/Media Center Website will continue to be updated with new links to support teaching activities. Logan would like to see the Web page building activity included as a supplemental contract area when her school's teaching contract is renegotiated.

Bringing It All Together and a Quick Guide to the E-library

Building a Web-based e-library is an ongoing process. This process will eventually include "weeding" and will always include "shelf-reading"—link checking and site verification in the Internet context. Hopefully, this book has given you the information and background you need to begin your Web-based e-library collection.

E-library Collection Maintenance and Management

In the past two years, it seems less likely to find that the person—or persons—collecting, selecting, and evaluating e-library resources is also maintaining the software and hardware through which the e-library is made accessible. The beginnings of this book are rooted in Chapter Four of a previous book written by the author for Neal-Schuman: *Cybrarians Guide to Successful Internet Programs and Services* (1997). That chapter discusses the planning, implementation, and maintenance of e-libraries with emphasis on the selection of software and hardware on which to make the e-library available rather than on collection development. Readers of the first book asked for more details about the collection development of e-libraries and reported less need for technical details, as those were being handled by Web server administrators or others. The e-library builder stories reported in this volume reflect that reality as well. So, maintenance of the e-library can be thought of in terms of "collection management" rather than Web server administration. E-library maintenance involves maintaining the quality and content of the e-library collection. This does not mean the e-library manager does not need to know anything about the technology. Below is a checklist that will help to guide you in planning and implementing e-library collection maintenance. The summary checklist is produced in table 7.2.

1. Stay in touch with the Web server administrator regarding software updates and changes.
   It is no joke that when upgrading software or hardware, Web server administrators may alter access to e-libraries by adding or deleting directories structures, changing input permission status for database access, and other related system changes. Developing and maintaining good communications with Web server administrators can ensure that you are not taken by surprise and that you will have input into any major changes that are planned.

2. Regularly review and check links in the e-library and/or select and use link-checking software such as Cyber Spyder Link Test or Linkbot.
   Checking links manually allows you to also review and verify that the Website not only still links properly but that it still provides the same information as it did when you originally annotated and added it to your e-library collection. It is recommended that you do this periodically, as things really do change or go away. Imagine your surprise if a library client discovers that the great kids' games and puzzles site you linked to is now a porn site. This is a true story and really happened to one of the e-library builders (who wishes to remain anonymous). Fortunately, the problem was discovered by a responsible adult before children were exposed to the changed site. Link checking software can be used for regular link-checking. It saves time, but it will only reveal to you whether the links are working and not whether the Websites have changed. Subscribe to Web4lib or search the archives to find other recommended link-checking software. Information about Cyber Spyder Link Test can be found at www.cyberspyder.com/ and for Linkbot at www.tetranetsoftware.com/. These two link-checkers were recommended by Web4Lib subscribers in Spring 1999. However you manage your links, check them frequently.

Table 7.2   An E-library Collection Maintenance and Management Checklist

1. Stay in touch with the Web server administrator regarding software up-dates and changes.
2. Regularly review and check links in the e-library and/or select and use link-checking software such as Cyber Spider Link Test (www.cyberspyder.com/) or Linkbot (www.tetranetsoftware.com/).
3. Provide a mechanism for e-library clients to evaluate and comment on the e-library Website contents and organization.
4. Review e-library Website organization and reorganize as necessary.
5. Review, update, and grow the contents of the e-library.

Dead links mean frustration for your clients and defeats the purposes of the e-library in providing good access to information.

3. Provide a mechanism for e-library clients to evaluate and comment on the e-library Website contents and organization; take their comments into consideration when reviewing organization of your Website.
    A simple mail to link or a Web form should be provided so that e-library clients can comment or evaluate the e-library contents and structure. This kind of feedback will allow you to make informed decisions about how well your e-library is serving your clients.

4. Review e-library Website organization and reorganize as necessary.
    For example, a review of the OPLIN e-library Website revealed a large number of resources under the broad category of "Business Informa-tion" under the sub-tropic of "International Business." It was decided to further organize those resources under sub-headings by continent (www.oplin.lib.oh.us/business).

5. Review, update, and grow the contents of the e-library.
    Content should always be reviewed on an ongoing basis. The only limi-tation to the growth of an e-library collection is disk space on the Web server and the time and energy of the collectors. Collection development tools for e-library collections continue to develop. New and better re-view sources, as well as new and better Web-based information sources, are made available literally every day. Limitations of time and the print medium have affected the specific review sources and resources show-

cased in the previous chapters. The Web itself provides a marvelous solution to this problem. This book's companion Website will continue to annotate and include new, or newly discovered, or recommended e-library collection development tools as well as additions to the Core Internet Ready-Reference Collections. Click on the link "Click Here to Be Added to the Mailing List for Updates and News" if you would like to be e-mailed when resources are added or updated.

Building a Web-based e-library may be the most important thing a library ever does. It demonstrates to our library clients and our communities and organizations that we are committed to fulfilling their information needs. It also represents a willingness to change and progress as the technological infrastructure of our international community and global economy shifts from the paper-based transmission and storage of information to the computer-based transmission and storage of information. The survival of libraries and the institution of librarianship is related to that willingness to progress and change. The maintenance of high standards of selectivity and information quality and an underlying philosophy of education and service have made librarianship an essential profession in the United States and around the world. Bringing that professionalism to the Internet we will certainly be welcomed as citizens—netizens—in the international community of the Internet.

Print and Electronic Publications Cited or Consulted in Chapter Seven

Bigham, V. S. and Bigham, G. 1998. *The Prentice Hall Directory of Online Education Resources*. New York: Prentice Hall Trade.

Castro, E. 1997. *HTML 4 for the World Wide Web: Visual QuickStart Guide*. Berkeley: Peachpit Press.

Glavac, M. 1998. *The Busy Educator's Guide To The World Wide Web*. London, Ontario: NIMA Systems.

Heide, A. and Stilborne, L. 1999. *The Teacher's Complete & Easy Guide to the Internet*. New York: Teachers College Press.

Kennedy, B., Loukides, M., Ed., and Musciano, C., 1997. *HTML: The Definitive Guide*. Cambridge, Mass.: O'Reilly & Associates.

Kovacs, D. K. and Kovacs, M. J. 1997. *Cybrarians Guide to Successful Internet Programs and Services*. New York: Neal-Schuman Publishers.

Leshin, C. B. 1998. *Internet Adventures: Version 2.0: Step-By-Step Guide to Finding and Using Educational Resources*. New York: Allyn & Bacon.

Webliographies Included with Chapter Seven

Education Resource Metasites

Academic Info
www.academicinfo.net
Contact: Mike Madin, index@academicinfo.net
Directory of Internet resources tailored to a college or advanced high school audience. Each subject guide is an annotated listing of the best general Internet sites in the field, as well as a gateway to more advanced research tools.

Ask Dr. Math
http://forum.swarthmore.edu/dr.math/

AskERIC ToolBox
http://ericir.syr.edu/Qa/Toolbox/
This is a collection of Internet resources that the network information specialists at AskERIC have found valuable when responding to teachers' questions.

Education Index
www.educationindex.com/
Contact: webmaster@educationindex.com
An annotated guide to the best education-related sites on the Web. They're sorted by subject and lifestage, so you can find what you're looking for quickly and easily. Lists more than 3,000 sites in 66 categories. Includes a chat room. Offered by CollegeView, a publisher of educational software.

Education Information Resources
www.educause.edu/ir/ir.html
Contact: info@educause.edu
Provides access to collections of materials related to managing and using information resources in higher education.

EdWeb
http://edweb.cnidr.org/
Contact: Andy Carvin, acarvin@gsn.org
Hyper-book relating to educational reform and information technology; a resource guide for k–12 online educational materials and discussion groups.

Eisenhower National Clearinghouse for Mathematics and Science
www.enc.org/
Contact: web@enc.org
Search for mathematics and science education materials.

InternetCurriculum Connection
www.ala.org/ICONN/curricu2.html
Contact: ICONnect@ala.org.
Integrating Internet resources into the curriculum; annotated high quality sites by subject (criteria explained).

Internet Scout Project
http://scout.cs.wisc.edu/scout/index.html
Contact: scout@cs.wisc.edu
Librarians and educators filter announcements and search weekly for online resources most valuable to the education community.

Kathy Schrock's guide for Educators
http://discoveryschool.com/schrockguide/index.html
Contact: Kathleen Schrock, MLS; kschrock@capecod.net
Critical evaluation for educators; categorized list of sites on the Internet found to be useful for enhancing curriculum and teacher professional growth.

Learning @ Web.Sites
www.ecnet.net/users/gdlevin/home.html
This site is a collection of annotated Websites intended for high school teachers' use in enhancing their instruction.

Mid-continent Regional Educational Laboratory
www.mcrel.org/standards-benchmarks/
Contact: info@mcrel.org
A compendium of standards and benchmarks for k–12 education.

Mid-continent Regional Educational Laboratory
www.mcrel.org/resources/
Contact: info@mcrel.org
Links to resources teachers can use in the classroom, as well as reports, articles, and directories that will help improve learning for all.

National School Network Exchange Web Site Evaluation
http://nsn.bbn.com/webeval/site1.htm
Contact: Jason, jravitz@bbn.com
Searchable database of reviewed educational Websites or enter a review of your own.

OH! Kids
http://oplin.lib.oh.us/products/oks/

Ohio Public Library Information Network's special e-library collection for kids.

Virtual Reference Desk – Ask A+ Locator
http://vrd.org/locator/index.html
Contact: vrd@vrd.org
Provides resources and links to experts (criteria explained) of different subjects relating to academics.

Virtual Search Engines
www.dreamscape.com/frankvad/search.html
Offers the most popular search engines and many specialized search engines (many annotated).

Yahooligans!
www.yahooligans.com/
Yahoo!'s special collection of homework and recreational Websites for kids.

Reader's Advisory/Collection Development Related Tools and Metasites

A Comparison of University Websites
http://riceinfo.rice.edu/~riddle/uniweb/
Contact: Prentiss Riddle, riddle@rice.edu
Easy-to-understand graphs compare Websites by size, graphics, techniques, structure, links, content, etc.

ACQLink
http://link.bubl.ac.uk/acqlink/
U.K. based Website which supports acquisition and collection development library activities.

ACQWEB
www.library.vanderbilt.edu/law/acqs/acqs.html
Website which supports acquisition and collection development librarians. Includes a listing of Web-based tools for non-Internet resource collection.

Amazon.com
http://amazon.com
Online bookstore that has searchable database of over 2.5 million books in and out of print.

American Libraries
www.ala.org/alonline/index.html
Visit the online version of the ALA's news publication. Besides providing all the news on libraries and librarians, articles about trends in spending and costs of publications appear here regularly.

Ariadne – The Web Version
www.ariadne.ac.uk/
Contact: Philip Hunter or Bernadette Daly, ariadne@ukoln.ac.uk
This newsletter describes and evaluates sources and services available on the Internet and of potential use to librarians and information professionals.

Booklist
www.ala.org/booklist/index.html
Contact: Bill Ott, bott@ala.org
This is the digital counterpart of the American Library Association's *Book List* magazine. It reviews thousands of the latest books (adult, children, reference), electronic reference tools, and audio-visual materials.

BOOK TV.org
www.booktv.org/
A great site for interviews with authors, summaries of books, and information on the publishing industry. Each weekend, "Book TV" on C-SPAN2 will feature 48 hours of nonfiction books from 8 a.m. Saturday to 8 a.m. Monday. This Website will enhance information on those books, provide an opportunity to watch or listen to programs you might have missed, and provide additional information not available on the cable network.

Collection Development Training for Arizona Public Libraries
www.dlapr.lib.az.us/cdt/index.htm
Web-based collection-development training published by the Arizona Department of Library, Archives, and Public Records.

College & Research Libraries News
www.ala.org/acrl/c&rlnew2.html
and/or
www.ala.org/acrl/resrces.html
Contact: Ann-Christe Young, ayoung@ala.org
Online version of magazine, some articles available online. Of specific interest are the Internet Reviews and Internet Resources (under departments).

Computer Policy & Law Collection
http://cuinfo.cornell.edu/CPL/Policies/

Contact: Computer Policy & Law Program, Cornell University, cpl-
    program@cornell.edu
Policy-making resources regarding security, privacy, guidelines, access, etc.
(12 types in all).

Criteria for the Selection of Full-Text Databases
www.snc.edu/~mankmm/criteria.htm
Contact: Michelle Manke, mankmm@mail.snc.edu
Provides criteria for your own collection-development decisions.

Digital Librarian
www.servtech.com/~mvail/new.html
Contact: Margaret Vail Anderson, mvail@servtech.com
Annotated listing and links to new (usually academic type, some "popular")
Websites.

Directory of Online Resources for Information Literacy
www.cas.usf.edu/lis/il/
Contact: Drew Smith, dsmith@luna.cas.usf.edu.
Database of sources regarding locating, evaluating and using information.

Directory of Scholarly and Professional Electronic Conferences
www.arl.org
or
www.n2h2.com/KOVACS
Contact: Diane K. Kovacs, MLS; diane@kovacs.com
Directory of discussion lists, newsgroups, mailing lists, chats, and MUDS which
have a scholarly or professional topic. Also published annually in print with
the ARL Directory of Electronic Journals as the *ARL Directory of Electronic
Journals Newsletters, and Academic Discussion Lists.*

The Discian Group
http://discian.com/
Contact: Kevin Eikenberry, info@discian.com
Provides reviews for organization trainers, consultants, and teachers; training
for success.

David Magier's Library World Bookmarks
www.columbia.edu/~magier/libworld.html
Contact: magier@intac.com
Categorized (outline format) databases relating to internet training and consulting.

Eric Lease Morgan's Professional Home Page
www.lib.ncsu.edu/staff/morgan/
Contact: Eric Lease Morgan, eric_morgan@ncsu.edu
Huge subject index on many relevant collection topics. Includes links to the
Alcuin Internet resource-cataloging project.

Glossary of bibliographic information by language
http://stauffer.queensu.ca/techserv/biblang.html
Terms are divided by language and do not appear in alphabetical order, but
with the use of your browser's "find in page" feature, this site should be easy
to use.

Glossary of Book Terms
www.abebooks.com/cgi/abe.exe/routera^progname=glossary
Offered by the Advance Book Exchange, this comprehensive list of terms is an
attempt to give definitions, in the most generic sense, that will apply to all or
most booksellers.

Government Information Quarterly
www.lib.auburn.edu/madd/docs/giq/title.html
Contact: WebManager@lib.auburn.edu
Includes reviews of government information-related resources.

HTML Writers Guild
www.hwg.org/
Contact: Homepage@hwg.org.
Provides assistance to Web authors. " . . . To compile and publicize information about standards, practices, techniques, competency, and ethics as applied
to Web authoring, and to contribute to the development of the Web and Web
technical standards and guidelines."

InFoPeople Project
www.infopeople.org/src/chart.html
Contact: Carole Leita, leita@infopeople.org
Charts of directories, search and metasearch engines, and the respective characteristics.

International Federation of Library Associations: Metadata Resources
www.ifla.org/II/metadata.htm
Contact: Terry Kuny, terry.kuny@xist.com
Digital libraries, metadata resources, articles, and discussions about many topics
relating to metadata.

The Internet Public Library – Book Reviews Serials
www.ipl.org/cgi-bin/reading/serials.out.pl?ty=long&id=ent0200
List of online journals that review books, videos, and other materials.

Internet Research News
www.researchbuzz.com/index.html
Contact: calumet@mindspring.com
Latest news and links to research Websites; search for a particular site; or subscribe to weekly e-mail resource listings.

Internet Resources Newsletter
www.hw.ac.uk/libWWW/irn/irn.html
Contact: Roddy MacLeod, senior faculty librarian; R.A.MacLeod@hw.ac.uk
A free newsletter for academics, students, engineers, scientists, and social scientists; useful round-up of new resources for academic users.

Internet Reviews Archive
www.bowdoin.edu/~samato/IRA
Contact: Sara Amato, samato@bowdoin.edu
College & Research Libraries News articles reviewing various Websites.

Internet Scout Net-happenings
www.scout.cs.wisc.edu/caseservices/net-hap/index.html
Contact: SusanCalcari, scal@cs.wisc.edu.
Comprehensive listing of 40–60 postings per day.

Internets
www.internets.com/
Contact: pgregor@internets.com
Largest filtered collection of useful search engines and newswires.

The Isaac Network Project
http://scout.cs.wisc.edu/scout/research/index.html
Contacts: Susan Calcari, project director; scal@cs.wisc.edu
Amy Tracy Wells, content coordinator; awel@cs.wisc.edu
Mike Roszkowski, technical coordinator; mfr@cs.wisc.edu
Information seeker's avenue to authoritative content, this project proposes to link geographically distributed collections of metadata into a virtual collection searchable as a unified whole.

LibraryLand: Collection Development: Resources
http://sunsite.berkeley.edu/LibraryLand/coll/soft.htm
Provides links to dozens of online book-reviewing sites.

Librarians' Site Du Jour
www.JennysCybrary.com/sitejour.html
Contact: jayhawk@wwa.com
Humorous annotated listing of sites; browse previous sites du jour.

Library Journal digital
www.bookwire.com/ljdigital/
Packed with news and summaries about new books in the Hot Picks,
Audiobook Reviews, Bestsellers, Book News, Pre Pub Alert, Video Reviews,
Database, and Disc Reviews sections.

Library Link
www.mcb.co.uk/liblink
Contact: Gillian Crawford, liblink@mcb.co.uk
The online information and discussion forum for librarians and information
professionals worldwide.

Library Web Manager's Reference Center
http://sunsite.berkeley.edu/Web4Lib/faq.html
Contact: SunSITE Manager, manager@sunsite.berkeley.edu
Directories, programs, tutorials, discussion topics, and links to digital library
maintenance, tools, and updates.

Libstats
http://libws66.lib.niu.edu/libstats/etst.htm
Libstats is designed to share local, state, and national library statistical reports electronically; provide examples of the types of library statistics being
reported; promote the use of library statistics; and provide information on
other Websites dealing with library statistics, data gathering, and reporting.
This site is being developed by Dr. Elizabeth Titus.

Metadata
www.ukoln.ac.uk/metadata/
Contact: Andy Powell, a.powell@ukoln.ac.uk
Reviews current approaches to resource description and looks at future options for metadata in the wider context of resource discovery.

Metadata Use in Libraries
http://library.kcc.hawaii.edu/mail-archives/metadata/
Contact: Bin Zhang, bzhang@hawaii.edu
Discussion group sorted by author, date, and thread.

Neat New Stuff We Found This Week
http://marylaine.com/neatnew.html
Contact: Marylaine Block, mblock@netexpress.net.
Listing of links of various choice sites with a comment about each.

Net Announce Articles from the Archives
www.erspros.com/net-announce/archive.phtml
Contact: Alicia Polk, alicia@erspros.com
Subscribers receive twice-weekly summaries of new Websites. This site lists (and links to) previously "announced" sites by last day, week, month, and year.

NetFirst Collection Development Policy
www.oclc.org/oclc/netfirst/nf960821.htm
Contact: OCLC, oclc@oclc.org
Framework for its policy development of its database.

Office of Research and Special Projects
www.oclc.org:5047/oclc/research/research.html
Contact: Eric J. Miller, emiller@oclc.org
Conference listings, research projects, and publications relating to resource management.

Phoaks
www.phoaks.com
Contact: thefolks@phoaks.com
Filtering project that looks through collection of Usenet newsgroups to find and extract messages about Internet resources. Opinions are read, classified, and tallied automatically.

Principles of Collection Management
http://adam.slis.lsu.edu/courses/7003
Contact: Dr. Dawson, NOTAED@LSUVM.SNCC.LSU.EDU
School of Library and Science Information's syllabus and handouts regarding collection policy

Publist
www.PubList.com/
Providing a centralized source of information on more than 150,000 of the world's periodicals. Its data comes from authoritative sources—*like R.R. Bowker's Ulrich's International Periodicals Directory & Trade*; and *Editor & Publisher International Yearbook®*—enhanced by helpful information and hyperlinks to participating publishers and secondary publishing services.

Publisher's Weekly.com
www.publishersweekly.com/
Lists and summaries of upcoming books, interviews with authors, and news about the publishing industry.

Reference Review Europe
www.rre.casalini.it/
Over 1,000 European reference book reviews online, full-text, searchable, and updated quarterly.

Sample Collection Policies for Electronic Resources
http://alexia.lis.uiuc.edu/~rrichard/RUSA/policies.html
Contact: rrichard@stripe.colorado.edu
Database of collection development policies.

Search Engine Watch
http://searchenginewatch.com
Contact: Danny Sullivan, http://searchenginewatch.com/about/comment.html
Database of search engine facts, guides, and resources.

Special Libraries Association
www.sla.org/index.html
Contact: Keith Collison, keith@sla.org.
Has an information resource center, publications, discussion lists, and research regarding special libraries.

Technology Information and Planning Site
http://nysernet.org/TIPS/home.html
Contact: TIPSter@nysernet.org
Informative first stop for school and library personnel implementing technology programs.

Technology Transfer Program
www.t2ed.com
Contact: Webmaster@t2ed.com
Technological materials for educational, internal, or commercial use.

Technical Processing Online Tools
http://tpot.ucsd.edu/
Contact: George J. Janczyn, gjanczyn@ucsd.edu
Library technical processing information resource; some restricted areas.

W3C Web Accessibility Initiative
www.w3.org/WAI/References/
Contact: Judy Brewer, jbrewer@w3.org
Highlights the work of organizations around the world in improving accessibility for people with disabilities.

WebTaxi
www.webtaxi.com
Contact: David Harper, dharper@donaudymunch.com
Includes a good list of search engines focusing on certain countries or regions, but not subject organization.

WebWatch
www.ljdigital.com/articles/multimedia/webwatch/webwatchindex.ASP
Contact: Paula Hammett, hammett@sonoma.edu
Monthly online review of the best Websites dealing with monthly subject.

What's New Archives
www.ncsa.uiuc.edu/SDG/Software/Mosaic/Docs/whats-new.html
Contact: Global Network Navigator, wn-comments@gnn.com.
Archive of early Websites (1993–1996).

What's New too!
http://nu2.com/
Contact: http://nu2.com/comments.html
Announcement service of new sites; no filters; updated daily.

Wired for Books
www.tcom.ohiou.edu/books/
Ohio University-sponsored site which provides book reviews and Realaudio readings!

University Library HTML Standards
http://library.csun.edu/reagan/
Contact: Michael Reagan, Internet database librarian; mreagan@csun.edu
This page has standards, lectures, and workshops relating to HTML standards, bibliography pages, and PowerPoint.

———

See **Collection Development Related Discussion Groups, E-serials and Guides, Evaluation Guides, and Workshops** Webliography in Chapter Two for discussion lists, newsgroups, e-serials, and other resources cited in this chapter.

Index

*The following typographical conventions are used in the index: **Boldface** identifies material contained in a Ready-reference Collection or a Webliography section of the book.